REVOLUTIONARY WAR VETERAN
William Keeble

OF

BLOUNT COUNTY
TENNESSEE

AND

HIS HEIRS

Albert W. Dockter, Jr.

HERITAGE BOOKS
2007

HERITAGE BOOKS

AN IMPRINT OF HERITAGE BOOKS, INC.

Books, CDs, and more—Worldwide

For our listing of thousands of titles see our website
at
www.HeritageBooks.com

Published 2007 by
HERITAGE BOOKS, INC.
Publishing Division
65 East Main Street
Westminster, Maryland 21157-5026

International Standard Book Number: 978-0-7884-4175-2

BOOK I

REVOLUTIONARY WAR VETERAN

WILLIAM KEEBLE OF BLOUNT COUNTY, TENNESSEE

AND HIS HEIRS

By: ALBERT W. DOCKTER, JR.

ACKNOWLEDGEMENTS

There are a great many people who have assisted me in the compilation of this book. To enumerate them all would be virtually impossible; however, with fear of overlooking someone, I will give thanks and appreciation to those most noteworthy.

I must give the original inspiration of starting the work to Mrs. Nancy Ellen Floyd Tarwater, daughter of Adaline Keeble Floyd and Richard B. Floyd. Her Daughter of the American Revolution Registration Number is #433651. It was she who had received copies of William Keeble's Revolutionary War record and permitted me to copy it in longhand.

Next in line for inspiration was Mr. Docie Keeble, who had a wealth of information about all the Keebles in the Blount County, Tennessee, area – living or dead – as he had made it a practice to attend any services where a Keeble was honored in any way. He had a loyalty to the family name, which was inspiring.

Mary Martin (Aunt Polly) Keeble Helton of Sevier County, in her nineties, had a clear and exacting mind. She could recall for us names and dates for the period following the Civil War when written documents were almost nonexistent. Her assistance was priceless.

All three of the above-mentioned were descendants of Thomas Keeble, firstborn of William and Mary Keeble.

A latecomer of this line was Mrs. Patricia Noble of Texas, whose ancestors had left Blount County prior to the Civil War, were burned out of their home in Chattanooga battlefield, and who fled to Rock Mills in southern Alabama – some of them later moving on to Texas. She wrote us seeking her "roots," and we could give her two more generations. Her help in enumerating all the Keeble generations since leaving Blount County was invaluable.

Those assisting me with the Manly Keeble line were brothers Dr. William H. and Edgar "Si" Keeble.

Of the Richard Keeble line were Mrs. Martha Adaline Keeble Perkins and Edward Simons of California. Mr. Simons has written up the Richard Keeble line after they left Blount County for California. A copy of his work is in the Maryville Public Library. Mrs. Clarinda Hatcher, a sister to Mrs. Perkins, assisted us in Blount County.

Doing a monumental task was Mr. Fred Beatty, who amassed the genealogy of the descendants of Walter Harrison Keeble family.

Coming down through the years (1950 - 2005) we had help and inspirations from Mrs. Marian Dunlap, Mrs. Bobbie Graves Young, Mrs. Myra French Williamson, and Mrs. Mary Ruth Rudd, the latter two pillars of the Keeble reunions each year in Rock Mills, Alabama.

To Mr. David H. Templin, who assisted me with Revolutionary and Civil War History and who assisted me in many ways throughout the years, I give thanks.

And last of all, my praise and gratitude to Mrs. Carolyn Yancey for taking my manuscript and typing and bringing it to fruition.

Albert W. Dockter, Jr., B.A.

Edgar Rhea Keeble (1893 – 1991)   Dorothy G. Dockter (1923 1982)

Mr. Edgar Rhea Keeble ("Si") and Mrs. Dorothy G. Dockter, both descendants of William Keeble, holding the rifle picked up by William Keeble on the Yorktown Battlefield at the surrender of General Charles Cornwallis on October 19, 1781.

This picture was taken on the front porch of Mr. Keeble's home on Keeble Street, Vestal, Knoxville, Tennessee, on November 7, 1975.

William Keeble presented the gun to his son Manly, who in turn gave it to his son Pleasant Marion Keeble. "Pleas" presented the gun to his youngest son, Edgar Rhea Keeble, who still had possession of the gun in November 1975.

The gun was passed down from generation to generation, with the understanding that it had to be given to a Keeble male.

Since Edgar Rhea Keeble had no children, he presented the gun to one of his brothers' sons prior to Edgar's death.

WILLIAM KEEBLE
SR.
MAY 23,1755
DEC.30,1834
A Revolutionary
Soldier and the first
owner of the soil that
now covers his remains

This book is dedicated to our three living children for whom it was originally instituted over a half century ago.

Helene Elaine Dockter Baker
Kathryn Diane Dockter West
Albert William Dockter and their progeny . . .

Albert W. Dockter, Jr.
2004

The Keeble Coat of Arms

Coats of Arms were developed in the Middle Ages as a means of identifying warriors in battles and tournaments. The present function of the Coat of Arms serves more to preserve the traditions that arose from its earlier use. The Keeble Coat of Arms - as described from a wax impression made in Middlesex County, Virginia, in 1698 and which had the following information regarding it.

"These Arms are somewhat similar to those of Sir Henry Keble, Knight Templar of Henry VIII whose daughter married William Browne, son and heir of Sir John Browne, Knight, Lord Mayor of London."

ARMS, Argent Chevron, engrailed gules on chief azure, three scallops of the field.

Crest: An elephant's head couped.

The authors' suggested meaning of this Coat of Arms: Three (es)callops of the field-symbolizing seafaring men. The elephant's head symbolizes the Keebles remarkably astute minds and memory.

A Grandmother's Legacy
By Patricia Keeble Noble
(11/23/1930 – 5/7/1991)

Summer has almost spent itself.
I can smell autumn in the crisp air
I do not know why,
But lately, I have been thinking of you,
My gossamer, young descendants
Who belong to the far distant future.

Is that not odd?
I have spent years of my life,
Obsessed by desire,
Searching, searching,
Arduously bending my mind, my will, my efforts,
Patiently sifting antiquated clues
To find my ancestors.
I treasure each small glimpse I can somehow find.

Lately though, I have been thinking of you.
Longing to see you clearly,
I peer at an impenetrable curtain.
Will one of you unknowingly have my smile?
Does one of you colonize some other planet?
Could one of you somehow change human destiny?
Or will you, on some far away summer day,
When you can smell autumn in the crisp air
Think of me and know that I thought of you?

INTRODUCTION

It was not long after I married Dorothy Kathryn Gredig in September 1945 that I learned that she and her ancestors in the Keeble line had been residents of Blount County, Tennessee, for several generations. That fact to me was remarkable, in that each generation of my own family had moved from one locale to another following their arrival from Europe.

Within four years, we had our first child, and I thought it appropriate to secure the baby's lineage, at least of the Keeble background. I considered it was entirely possible that we might move to another location and the opportunity might never present itself for securing that information again.

With the help of Mr. Docie Keeble, a wonderful friendly man who himself had kept up with all the Keebles attending weddings, funerals, family reunions, anyone with the name KEEBLE, I started acquiring knowledge and information about the family.

He had the Bible of Thomas Keeble, the firstborn of the union of William and Mary Keeble. It was a leather-bound volume upon which he stated his father had honed his straight razor. Docie permitted me to copy all the information from it (the Xerox machine had not yet been invented). He then gave me all the direct descendants from William and Mary Keeble leading down to my wife and child.

At that early time, I had six generations from a Revolutionary War Veteran. The acquisition of facts seemed simple and rewarding. Then started the search for the parents of William Keeble. It is now fifty years later and I still do not know who his parents were for a certainty. I had always said "As soon as I am able to identify Williams' parents, I will write the book." That time has never arrived to date.

Dotty was a big help in my search. When we drove to New York State to visit my folks, we would stop in Warrenton, Virginia, County seat of Fauquier County from whence William and Mary came, to search for information. The beautiful old courthouse still stands, but many of the old records had deteriorated and were not available for our perusal.

9

We were able to find Mary Keeble's father and mother's records, she also being a Keeble prior to her marriage, the marriages of her brothers and sisters, and a few land transactions, but nothing on William's ancestry.

We spent time in Maryland Hall of Records, the Virginia and West Virginia state libraries, New York and Tennessee state libraries, the McClung collection in Knoxville, and all the surrounding county courthouses securing vital statistics on the Keeble family. Dotty, the children, and I spent many hours in cemeteries securing names and dates we needed to complete family records.

As a former Yankee going into the recesses of the mountains around Maryville, I learned (in my insurance adjusting profession) that the mountain people were not overly zealous in communicating with people they didn't know. I learned to advise those with whom I had to communicate that I was married to Dotty Gredig, granddaughter of Laban Keeble, and a distant attitude suddenly became friendly. In this way I was able to function as an adjuster and also in my search for genealogy. Laban Keeble had worked most of the days of his life at Peerys' Mill in Walland, Tennessee. Walland, a rural farming area and at one time the site of a tanning factory for the curing and processing of hides, bordered Little River and Perrys' Mill received its power from water pressure gained by a dam across the river.

The surrounding community was of an agricultural nature, and all roads led to the mill where farmers had their grains and corn ground and were thus acquainted with Mr. Keeble.

When I had a claim in the vicinity of any of the "old timers" of the Keeble clan, I made it a point to seek them out and get what information I could from them. My, what I would give now to have had a tape recorder and been able to transcribe the wealth of information that poured from their lips...their quaint expressions and their complete honesty in relating what they could of the family.

Some of the first folk interviewed remembered the children of William Keeble, Revolution War Veteran. If only I had had the time to sit and copy all that they had to tell, about being "hexed" by a cow or hearing one sing a childhood song that they had made up about William's children in their old

10

age. The song gave an unbiased expose of the children, then old, revealing their attitudes of their elders from a bygone era.

None of these personages could tell us the background of William. We had his Will from the courthouse in Maryville, Blount County, Tennessee. He left $1.00 each to his four children from an earlier union. They were listed by name but no information about where they lived.

William stated in his Will that there would be an inheritance from both his mother and father's side of the family but did not identify who the parents were or where their property was located.

Two of the elders said that as children they would enter a room and realize that there was a discussion about William's background in progress; but with the arrival of "young ears," the conversation ceased and the children never learned the secret.

We must assume at this late date that the conversation concerned the four black children sired by William and his slave Sarah. Perhaps the second generation did not wish the grandchildren of William to know about the existence of these children (pure conjecture on my part).

We have found Keebles in Maryland from the 1600s on. The given names of these folks are very similar to William's family.

We heard early on that there were two Keeble Bibles, one Marys and the other Williams. If this is true, the latter one has never come to light. It certainly could solve a lot of secrets many of us have been pondering for over fifty years.

So we will search on and hope that sometime we or our descendants will find the clues that will enable us to link the three Maryland Wills with our William.

BOOK I
TABLE OF CONTENTS

APPENDIX

WILLS – SOMERSET COUNTY, MARYLAND

November 24,1998

To Whom It May Concern:

I,Dr.Elmer E.Mize,aged 70,of 615 Washington Street in
Maryville,Tennessee,37804,have been the sole Editor of
the BLOUNT JOURNAL,the official publication of the Blount
County Genealogical and Historical Society since its
inception in 1955.
Mr.Albert W.Dockter,Jr.has contributed numerous articles
for publication in the JOURNAL with the understanding by
me that the articles given to me for publication were to
be reproduced in his forthcoming genealogy of the KEEBLE
FAMILY OF BLOUNT COUNTY,TENNESSEE.
I accepted those articles in their entirety with the
understanding that the copyright laws wouldnot hinder Mr.
Dockter from re-producing the articles in his volume.

Signed this 25th day of November,1988

Elmer E. Mize
Dr.Elmer E.Mize,Phd.

A

WILLIAM KEEBLE

To say the background of William Keeble of Blount County, Tennessee, is shrouded in obscurity is the understatement of the century. Numerous genealogists have attempted to ascertain his background prior to the Revolutionary War and indeed from the War up until the time of his marriage to Mary Keeble in 1799. All sources of information usually available for the genealogist are nonexistent or have been meticulously eradicated. For example:

1. William Keeble's personal family Bible has disappeared.
2. Bible records copied in Somerset, Maryland, by a Mrs. Magruder and forwarded to the Daughters of the American Revolution in Washington cannot be located.
3. The Record Book of Leeds Parish, Fauquier County, Virginia, which would have contained the family names of the Parish, the birth, marriage, and death dates, as well as lineage of the Keebles, was destroyed according to the last Vicar of the Parish at the Fauquier County Courthouse after the Vicar was moved and no new Vicar appointed.
4. A courthouse record of a lawsuit brought in 1786 by Betty Leach against William Keeble in Chancery Court of Fauquier County is known only because the "jacket" the suit was stored in is still in existence, BUT the contents of the jacket are gone.
5. William Keeble himself withheld information from his children which would have assisted his heirs in determining who their grandparents were and from whence they came.

These are but a few of the frustrations I encountered in searching the lineage. If it had not been for William and Mary's determination in seeking pensions from the United States government, a search of William's past would have been futile.

The facts that we have otherwise are meager, but I shall attempt to give his life story as best I can, calling upon written facts and family traditions from the different branches of the family as told to me.

It has always been my supposition that the Keebles were of English origin. W. H. Keeble, great grandson of William, stated in a letter to me the following, "My father remembered that his father, Manly, stated that the first

Keeble came to this country from England and that he crossed the Atlantic several times. (Was he a sailor, or was his business important enough to take him to England on business?)

I think it is a reasonable inference that George Keeble was our ancestor. Middlesex County is at the mouth of the Rappahannock River, which is navigable for fairly large boats as far up as Fredericksburg. It is my theory that some of George's descendents traveled by boat up the Rappahannock River and traveled overland into Prince William County some forty or fifty miles from Fredricksburg. (Fauquier County was carved out of Prince William County.) Our William and Mary Keeble came from Fauquier County. Judging by the date of _____, the George Keeble deed, and the date of William Keeble's birth (1755), George could have been William's grandfather."

In corresponding with descendants of one John Keeble of Fauquier County and whose son Richard B. Keeble was living in St. Charles County, Missouri, in 1850, their family tradition indicated that the first Keebles in the New World settled in Maryland for several generations and then migrated to Virginia.

Certainly there were Keebles in Somerset County, Maryland, in the 1600s. Records tend to show that George Keeble was a ship captain plying the high seas between England and the Colonies. Captain Keeble received land for each indentured servant he brought to the colonies, and they in turn worked for him for seven years to pay for their fare across the waters. Upon the land he secured in this way, he planted tobacco and it was tended by these indentured servants.

Returning to England with tobacco, Keeble could purchase supplies to ferry more prisoners or others wishing to come to the colonies and thus secure more land for himself. George Keeble had quite a number of plots of land in Maryland.

We have the Wills of three generations of Keebles from Somerset County, Maryland. They are placed in the back of this book. It is interesting to realize that these men had property enough to write Wills protecting their offspring.

Had the Keebles overworked the land and was there promise of richer soil in Virginia, perhaps religious controversy, or possibly of a devastating hurricane (such as we have seen from time to time ravaging the coast) which caused the Keebles to move inland? Somerset county, Maryland, is but thirty or forty miles from the Atlantic Coast. The low land was subject to storms and flooding. For some reason, they opted to relocate in Virginia.

The three Somerset County Wills of William Keeble, William Keeble, Sr., and George Keeble were written in 1727, 1770, and 1775, respectively.

The Stepney P. E. Register in Maryland mentions several Kibble marriages and offspring of those marriages. Unfortunately, most of the records are of the distaff side of the families but do furnish us with some of the names of who the Keebles married:

- Richard Biglands married Mary Kibble on March 22, 1749/50. Their children are listed.
- Jarvis Jenkins married Sarah Kibble on January 29, 1744/5. One of their children was named Kibble Jenkins.
- Thomas Price married Patience Kibble on December 22, 1756.
- Patience Kibble, daughter of John Kibble and Sarah, his wife (B:9/25/1738).
- Anne Stevens Kibble, daughter of William Kibble and his wife Hannah (B:1/1/1746).
- Sarah Kibble, daughter of William Kibble and Hannah, his wife (B:9/18/1748).
- Job Shermon married Abagail Kibble on February 5, 1733. Their children listed.
- John Kibble, son of William Kibble and Hannah, his wife (B:4/6/1763).
- William Kibble was married to Elizabeth Stewart on July 24, 1763.
- William Collins, son of Thomas Collins and Rebecca, his wife, married to Emme Kibble on October 10, 1782. Their son is listed.
- William Kibble, son of John Kibble and Elizabeth, was born October 10, 1792.

Thus we see that Keebles were in Maryland up through the birth of our William. Certainly the given names of the Maryland Keebles continue on with the Virginia families. I cannot connect the families with the information on hand, but the St. Charles, Missouri, family tradition would tend to confirm the succession of generations from Maryland to Virginia. In corresponding with a Mrs. Travis Keeble from Lakeport, California, we learned that James Travis Keeble's father, Alfonzo Travis Keeble (born in 1881), had the following history tradition of the Keebles.

"The first Keeble came from Ireland, date unknown . . . during the time of the Campbells. They settled in Maryland. The number of generations in Maryland, unknown. There were two sons. One branch of the family – unknown - migrated to the southern states. It is possible it was Kentucky because it is known that there are Keebles there. The other son moved to Virginia – name unknown – had a son Richard Bradley Keeble (1800-1862). Richard B. born in Virginia, and had four sons: Cumberland, William, Alfonzo, and Richard Best Keeble. Richard Best K. (1853-1925) went to Missouri. He had two sons: Alfonzo Travis Keeble (1881) and Ray (1891). Alfonzo Travis (1881) had two sons: Richard Burks (1917) and James Trave (1922). Ray (1891) had three sons: Raymond (1922), Kenneth (1924), and Hal (1928). These Keebles had roots in Fauquier County, Virginia, as there are court records linking Keebles in Missouri with Anderson Keeble in the sale of land in Fauquier County. My correspondence with the Trave Keebles was in 1951.

There were several family traditions which I heard repeated numerous times from the descendants of William's children. The first tradition was that the Keebles came to America from Scotland. One branch of the family even stated that William's middle name was McDonald. I have never seen William Keeble's name written with a middle initial or name. I have never seen any proof of Scotland being the origin of the family, other than hearing Ella Floyd Tarwater state it and including it in her resume to the Daughters of the American Revolution for entry into their ranks.

The second tradition is that William Keeble played with George Washington as a child. This hardly seems possible in that George was born in 1732 and William in 1755. However, it is quite possible that William's father, who was also William and the elder William, may have known George. There were William Keeble Sr., and Jr., in Fauquier County in 1790. In any event, we know that Mr. Washington owned land in Fauquier County and complained that while he was away commanding the Continental Troops, someone had built a mill on his property in Fauquier.

The third tradition relates that William had two brothers, Cumberland and Alfonzo. The three brothers were said to have fashioned log rafts in

Saltville, Virginia, loaded the rafts with salt, and floated down the rivers and streams to the frontier where they sold the salt and returned overland on foot to Saltville where they repeated the venture. It is interesting to me that Docie Keeble had the names CUMBERLAND and ALFONZO in his memory.

The St. Charles Missouri branch of the family had both Cumberland and Alfonzo listed as given names, but nowhere in our lineage were these names ever used. If there is any truth to the story of salt transportation and our William was involved, perhaps he had already seen the area to be known as Blount County and had made a decision to come here when settlement in this area was possible.

It is interesting to note that the Leeds Parish Area of Fauquier County, Virginia, backs up to the mountain range just as the Walland area of Blount County backs up to the Smoky Mountain range. The better land of Fauquier County was level and had already been settled before the Leeds Parish Area was created from Hamilton Parish.

Another tradition comes to mind, the story that William Keeble sired 22 children. We can account for fifteen of them with our records. It is quite possible that in that day and time the other children may have been stillborn or infant deaths occurred and they had been unnamed. There is only one of the fifteen-named children who we know nothing about (Harriett), who may have fit into the category or who died young like her namesake (Harriett), sister of Mary.

I should state that in Maryland, as well as Virginia, the Keeble name was spelled variously – Keeble, Kibble, Keible, Keble, and once or twice Cable. Sometimes the various spellings were in the same document.

We have a copy of William's war records, as given by the Department of the Interior in 1922. In William Keeble's application for a pension, he gave in detail the history of his service. From his Declaration to obtain benefits of the Act of Congress passed the 18th day of March in 1818 and subscribed by William on June 6, 1818, he states that he enlisted about the year 1776 in Fauquier County, Virginia, in the Company of Captain James Scott in a Regiment commanded by Colonels Toliver and Stephens and Major Thomas Marshall for the term of one year as a private soldier. He was in the battle of Long Bridge, Virginia, and was subsequently discharged. At that time, he would have been 21 years of age. Then in August of 1777, he again enlisted in Fauquier County in Captain Elias Edmonds Company of the Artillery of Colonel Thomas Marshall's Regiment in the Line of the State of Virginia on the Continental Establishment. He served as a Bombadier and was discharged in Richmond, Virginia, on August 22, 1780 (this is the same time John Marshall resigned his commission). He further states that in 1781, he was in the Militia Service at the Siege of York and the capture of Cornwallis. (It was on this field of battle that he picked up a musket which he brought home and is still the prized possession of the descendants of Manly Keeble, his son, to whom he gave it.)

Late in the fall of the year 1781 just before Christmas, he enlisted in Captain Beverly Ray's Company in the Regiment commanded by Major Finley and Colonel Posey and marched to the south where he was in the battle of the "defeat and death of Gurister Sigo-the Indian Chief" about four miles south of Savannah, Georgia. He was also in several skirmishes and late in the fall of 1782, they were marched back to Cumberland old Courthouse, Virginia, where they were again honorably discharged. He was now about 27 years of age.

William was living in Blount County, Tennessee, when he made this Declaration. He needed someone to attest to its authenticity, so he took a friend, James Kennard, who had been in the second of the campaigns for a term of three years mentioned above and who was living here in Blount County in 1818.

Throughout this book, one will find references to some clandestine event or events that always concerned the grandchildren about William Keeble's past. We have spent years attempting to determine if that event was of a legal nature, a moral deception, the stealing of a birthright, an allegiance to the King of England, the slaying of someone – we had not a clue.

You will note in William's Will drawn up four days before his death that his negro slave Sarah is in his household. In his Declaration of 1829, William states that Sarah is about sixty years of age. This would have made her birth year approximately 1769; and in 1782, she would have been about thirteen years of age. Where William secured this slave we have not a clue. Perhaps she was inherited from his family estate.

With the publication of a book (1999), "The Taxman Cometh" (tax lists from the Fauquier County Court Clerks Loose Papers 1759-1782 compiled by John W. Peters C.G.R.S on page 89, we find a possible explanation of the secrecy regarding William's past that perhaps his children wished to keep from the grandchildren in that day.

As you will note on page 77, Mr. William Healy of Fauquier County, Virginia, was appointed to gather the tax list for Leeds Parish in Fauquier County in 1782. A Parish was an area of land in which the borders were designated by the Episcopal Church and in which the inhabitants of that area went to church, paid their tithes, and whose family births, marriages, and deaths were recorded in the Parish Register.

William Keeble was a member of the Parish of Leeds simply by residing in that area. You will note in Mr. Healy's 1782 tax list for William Keeble we find:

> William Keeble
> N. (Negro) Sarah D*(Daughter) Sarah young
> 1 Horse 1 Cow

In William's Will, he states that he has four children whom he leaves one dollar apiece. Now we go to the 1787 tax list for Fauquier County, which is also revealed on page 275. This tax list was taken on March 10, 1787.

Look for William Keeble in the lower chart and you will see under Item 2 a (1) is listed Under Item 3 a (4) is listed. Item #2 refers to Sarah the slave, Item #3 refers to the number of Blacks under 16 years of age in the household. Thus we know that during the years from 1782-1787, William Keeble and his slave Sarah begat the four children mentioned in his Will. In the Will, he calls Sarah "Sally," which was a common nickname for Sarah in that day. He listed the children (possibly in order of birth) Sally, William, John, and Nancy. William does give us a clue that perhaps Nancy is already deceased (1834), for he states "Nancy or her heirs," which might preclude her demise.

Some historians state that between the years of 1700-1875, there were "Naming Patterns" for children, although these naming patterns were not universally used in order of birth in a family. The first son was named for his paternal grandfather; the second son was named for his maternal grandfather; the first daughter born was named for her maternal grandmother; and the second daughter was named for her father's mother. If William and Sarah followed this naming pattern, William's father would have been William. Sarah's father would have been John.

THE PERSONAL PROPERTY TAX LIST FOR THE YEAR 1782 FOR FAUQUIER COUNTY, VIRGINIA
Copyrighted material used by the author with written permission of Joan W. Peters, C. G. R. S. from "The Tax Man Cometh," Pg. 89

<u>1782-004 WILLIAM HEALE'S PROPERTY LIST</u>
A List of Property taken by Wm Heale
[page 13]

Person's Names and all Names of Negroes	White Tithes Above 21	White Tithes Under 21	Negro Tithes	# Negroes	# Horses	Cattle	Wheels	Billiard Tables	Ordinary Licenses
Kibble, John Anderson Kibble, un^r 21	1	1			2	6			
Kibble, Wm N. Sarah, D° [Sarah] young. 1 horse, 1 Cow	1			1	1	1			

THE PERSONAL PROPERTY TAX LIST FOR THE YEAR 1787 FOR FAUQUIER COUNTY, VIRGINIA
Copyrighted material used by the author with written permission of Netti Schreiner-Yantis from "The 1787 Census of Virginia" for Fauquier County, Pg. 295, Tax List "C"

Form of return of taxable property to be made by the commissioners.

List of taxable property within the district of A. B. commissioner in the county of O—, for the year 1787

Date of receiving lists from individuals	Persons names, chargeable with the tax.	Names of white male tithables above 21.	Number of white males above 15 and under 21.	Blacks above 16	Blacks under 16.	Horses, mares, colts & mules	Cattle.	Carriage wheels	Ordinary licences	Billiard tables.	Neat/usual horses.	Rates of covering prices on	Practising physicians, apothecaries-rrica-licer geons.
1787. 10	A. C.	A C	1	2	3	4	5	2	1	1	1	£.2 0 0	
March10 11	A. D.	AD&EF	"	1	2	1	3	"	1	"	"	0 0 0	
12	A. E.	A E.	"	"	"	"	0	"	"	"	"	0 0 0	
10	B. F.	BF & IK	2	10	15	9	30	8	"	"	2	5 0 0	
12	C. G.	C G	"	15	10	10	25	"	1	"	"	0 0 0	
13	D. H.	D H	3	"	1	2	7	"	1	1	"	0 0 0	
	Total amount. 9		6	28	31	26	70	8	4	2	3	7 0 0	

1.   2.   3.   4.   5.

Fauquier County Personal Property Tax 1787 - List "C"

Last Name	First Name	Charged with Tax	1	2	3	4	5	Notes
								- 16-21 yrs.
Roach	George	Isham Keith	0	1	0	1	2	
Kinkead	Wm.	self	0	0	0	1	2	
Kibble	James	self	0	0	0	1	6	
Kirkpatrick	Wm.	self	0	1	4	1	3	
Kibble	William	self	0	0	0	1	0	
kincheloe	James	self						

A

I.   William Keeble   First Family   Slave Sarah
     B: 5/21/1755   B: / / Abt. 1769
     D: 12/30/1834   D: / / Aftr. 1834

II. Children: Sally, John, William, Jr., Nancy

     Sally Keeble   M: / /   _____
     _____
     B: Abt. 1780   B: / /
     D: / /   D: / /

     William Keeble, Jr. M: / /   _____
     B: / /   B: / /
     D: / /   D: / /

     Nancy Keeble.   M: / /   _____
     B: / /   B: / /
     D: / /   D: / /

     John Keeble.   M: / /   _____
     B: / /   B: / /
     D: / /   D: / /

In several of the personal property tax lists of Fauquier County 1782-1786, a John Keeble lived with William. From 1787 to 1799 both men are listed but no longer living together. In the year 1800, William is no longer listed, as he had left for Tennessee in the spring of 1800.

I do not know if the first four children were left in Virginia or came to Tennessee with their mother and father. Sally would have been about 18 years old, the others younger. One would assume they were brought along to the new territory. As blacks, they had no legal status.

I find no marriages for these children in Blount County other than a John Keeble who married a Catherine Ledbetter in 1819. Catherine was already a widow, and so we don't know her maiden name. Her former husband was Lewis Ledbetter.

There is mention of a William Keeble at an early date who helped as a chain bearer when William Keeble's land was surveyed. The owner of the land could not help in the survey, and so this William Keeble may be an assistant in the survey. I have no idea if a person of mixed blood was permitted to assist in a chore of this kind.

One wonders why William left these first four children a dollar each. Possibly it was to all of his lawfully born children to share and share alike. He also stipulated that if there was any inheritance to come from his wife Mary's parents, it should be divided amongst her lawfully born children. In this way, the first four children were not ignored apparently. I should state that John Keeble was a Veteran of the War of 1812 in the East Tennessee Militia. His government record is given in a chapter at the rear of the book. I have no proof that he was a child of Sarah and William Keeble.

One must remember that Thomas Jefferson had a similar relationship with his slave Sally Hemings. Both men, William and Thomas Jefferson, were from the same state, almost the same time period (Jefferson died in 1826 and William in 1834), and they lived perhaps sixty miles apart. Their slaves were their property. Jefferson had five children by Sally Hemings.

When William died in 1834, Sarah was still living. In his Will, he advised Sarah to stay with Mary until Mary died and then she had the privilege of choosing which of the children she wished to live with. Sarah would have been 86 years of age when Mary died in 1855, thus she probably was already buried in the Keeble graveyard without a marker.

It is common knowledge that in that day (1820-1830), individuals of mixed blood usually went to the frontier where their time was consumed in eking out a living and there was little time for social criticism of their plight as mulattoes.

In 1784 William was issued a Land Office Military Warrant (#2477) for "Land set aside for officers and soldiers of the Commonwealth of Virginia." On February 11, 1784, the Warrant issued 200 acres to Keeble for his three years in the Virginia State Line.

Apparently at the time, William was not interested in moving to Greenbriar County, which at that time was in Virginia but is now West Virginia, so he sold his Warrant for the 200 acres to one Daniel Feagan for a sum of money. Feagan apparently went about buying up the Warrants from the recipients to acquire the land.

There was a tradition in the family that I failed to mention earlier. It was told that William had a brother, James, who was in the service with William during one of the three enlistments. Docie Keeble, mentioned in the introduction, stated that William had a brother James who came to Blount County, but all records of this man appear lost.

Adding to the author's dilemma is the knowledge that the State of Tennessee issued a Warrant for "a" James Keble, Deceased, on June 24, 1824, for 274 acres of land in the Thirteenth District of Gibson County, Tennessee, for his services in the Revolutionary War for the State of North Carolina.

Docie mentioned that some of James' children came to Maryville a couple of generations ago seeking information about their parent, James Keeble. We have a copy of the letter written by one of the children seeking their father's backpay and veterans rights February 3, 1831, to Mr. Robert Green:

"Sir, I understand that you are going to Richmond for the purpose of making an examination into the Revolutionary Claims. I desire that you will see whether there ever was a Warrant issued in my fathers' name for his military service during the Revolutionary War as a soldier in the Virginia line, if not-cause the same to issue and bring to his heirs. He enlisted in the company commanded by Elias Edmonds and was in the Regt. Commanded by Col. Morgan and I also understood from him in his lifetime that he never got his monthly pay for about three years of the time he enlisted for during the war. Draw his money and interest for the same and you will confer a particular favor on me. Yours, Respectfully, James Keeble (for himself and his heirs) of James Keeble, Dec'd. " It was among the Rejected Claims on March 11, 1831.

Miss Inez Burns, author of the book The History of Blount County, Tennessee from the War Trail to Landing Strip had a James Keeble listed in the Roster of Revolutionary Soldiers in the first edition of her book. However, this name was deleted from subsequent editions. We feel reasonably sure that James Keeble was at one time here in Blount County and purported to be William's brother. In 1783 a James Keeble was granted a Land Office Treasury Warrant (#18171) DATED July 23, 1783, for 66 acres of land situated in Greenbrier County, Virginia, on Howard's Creek and adjoining the lands of heirs of Levin Gibson, deceased. One of Mr. Levin Gibson's daughters was Charlotte Gibson Keeble, wife of James Keeble. In a Land Office Treasury Warrant (#4948) surveyed October 12, 1812, the heirs of Levin Gibson, deceased, were granted 100 acres of land on the headwaters of Howards Creek. One would imagine these acres were granted earlier and were surveyed in 1812, also in Greenbriar, Virginia.

Warrants of this James Keeble and Levin Gibson do not appear to be of a military nature. I cannot understand the numbering system of the latter two warrants and their dates of inception.

William Keeble was born May 21, 1755, as recorded in Mary Keeble's Bible, Mary Keeble being the wife of William. His place of birth is unrecorded. It is my assumption that he was probably born in Somerset County, Maryland, and the three Wills of William Keeble, William Keeble, Sr., and George Keeble recorded in Somerset County, Maryland, and recorded in the back of this book were our William's direct ancestors.

William Keeble's chronological wartime service record is as follows. Our first real proof of his location is in reference to his enlistment in the Revolutionary War from the State of Virginia, County of Fauquier, for one year, which was presumably from 1775-1776, when he was twenty years of age. He was a Private and was at the battle of Long Bridge in Virginia and was honorably discharged at the completion of his year's service. He then re-enlisted in August 1777 for three years and again was honorably discharged in Richmond, Virginia, on August 22, 1780.

While it is not a tradition of the family, it is known that William Keeble was born the same year as a man who would later become the first Chief Justice of the Supreme Court of the United States – John Marshall. John Marshall was born in 1755 in Fauquier County, Virginia, and was an officer "over" Keeble in the Revolutionary War. John Marshall resigned his Commission in 1780 and returned to Fauquier County to practice Law. This is at the same time Keeble, as stated above, was discharged at Richmond.

It is interesting that the first case that distinguished John Marshall was the case of Hite vs. Fairfax (1786), in which he successfully upheld the claims of the tenants of Lord Fairfax to that part of northern Virginia, known as "The Northern Neck." Indeed, he may have been defending some of the land that John Keeble had rented from Lord Fairfax.

In the year 1781, William was in the Militia Service at the siege of York and witnessed the capture and surrender of Lord Cornwallis. Late in the same year (1781) just before Christmas, he enlisted in a Regiment and marched south and was in the defeat of an Indian Chief about four miles south of Savannah, Georgia. William referred to the Chief as "Old King Sago," but I assume that is what he "made out" of the pronunciation of "Gurister Sigo." In the fall of 1782, he marched back to Cumberland Old Courthouse in Virginia and was again honorably discharged. He was now 27 years of age.

We know that a Humphrey Keeble and a Walter Keeble were living in Cumberland County at this time and wonder if William visited his kinfolk after being discharged at that location. They were descendants of the Gwinn Island, Virginia Keebles.

Through an uncanny series of events, I happened upon a roster of William Keeble's Regiment led by Colonel Marshall (son of John). This is the group which apparently continued on until after the defeat and capture of Lord

Cornwallis at Yorktown. In it are several names of interest in William's later life.

In the Declaration of William Benson, Revolution War Vet. In applying for a pension, we find a list of the fellow soldiers in William Keeble's unit of service. Mr. Benson describes it as follows: He "was a soldier in Col. Marshall's Regiment of the Artillery at Yorktown. He and John Hammonds made this list. Elias Edmonds, crenel. Poor dear Colonel Edmonds, the last time I seed him was at Faquier courthouse, and we drank some grog together for the last time that I ever seed him in this world, or ever shall again. He has gone to the other world."

"Elias Edmonds, Capt. Of Company U.S. A.
Samuel Blackwell, Leutennant

Vallentine Leach
George Leach Sener
George Leach Juner
James Jones
Daniel Cornwel
John Porter
Hendley More
Peter Moore
William Kibble
James May
Joseph Weedon
George Bullet
Enoch Smith
William Waddle
Jacob Gipson
Joshua Drummond
Joshua Kennard
James Kennard
John Thornton
Reuben Thornton
Thom. Jett
John Hammonds

William Benson
John Mcall
James Mclannahan
James Boothe
John Ridley
John Area
Bennet Wats
Mason Wats
Joseph Markwell
Peter Hitt
Nathan Holtzclaw
Benjamin Utterback
William Higgins
John Higgins
Enoch Foley
Andrew Smith
Thomas Hudnal
Thomas White
Zachariah Tayler
William Rice
William Haney
Benjamin Piper

Land-Office Military Warrant. No. I 2477

To the principal SURVEYOR of the Land, set apart for the Officers and Soldiers of the
Commonwealth of Virginia.

THIS shall be your WARRANT to survey and lay off in one or more
surveys, for

Daniel Feagan ass.ee of William Kibble

his Heirs or Assigns; the Quantity of *two hundred*

Acres of Land, due unto the said *Daniel Feagan*
Kibbles

in consideration of *the said* Services for *three years as as Corporal*
in the Virginia state line

agreeably to a Certificate from the Governor and Council, which is received into the Land-Office.

GIVEN under my Hand, and Seal of the said Office, this *11th*
February in the Year, One Thousand Seven Hundred and *84* Day of

A

We know that of this group of men, besides Kibble, James Kennard, whose wife attended William and Mary's wedding, lived in Blount County, Tennessee, for a time.

It is interesting to note the following details from Mr. Benson's file. "This is to certify that William Benson a soldier in Col. Marshall's Regiment of Artiullery have due him from the State of Virginia one coate, one vest, one pr. Breeches, two shirts, two pr. Stockings, two pr. Shoes and one hatt. The Virginia Auditor reported that William Benson, soldier of artillery was paid L77.15.6 in full on 24 June 1783."

One would assume that William Keeble, being in the same Regiment, would have had a similar mustering out payment and clothing allotment.

We do know that in November of 1799, William Keeble and William Sutton purchased a schooner boat, "The Greyhound," from one Wilson White. It was purchased for $140. Unfortunately, we do not know the site of the purchase of the schooner boat. However, the Rappahannock River has its source in the Blue Ridge Mountains, just west of Fauquier County. In fact, the Rappahannock River is one of the borders of Fauquier County. We are told that where the river empties into the Chesapeake Bay, the river is affected by the ocean tides 100 miles upstream. This water course was the route of travel for the two Williams as they sailed to Maryland in November 1799 and upon their return to Virginia the same month. The boat was then titled in William Suttons name. These transactions were recorded in both Maryland and Virginia State papers.

In taking an "Overview" of the relationship of the Maryland and Virginia Keebles and without proof to back it up at the present time, I believe our William was a close kin to the Maryland family because:

(1)   The purchase of the schooner boat in November of 1799, one month prior to William's marriage, would tend to prove that his intentions were to move inland to Tennessee, and it would be his last chance to personally determine the condition of the estates he later advised he knew were due him as heir of his mother and father's legacies.

(2)   There are marriages recorded in Somerset County, Maryland, which include two Keebles who may be the children of William's first family.

The years of these marriages would possibly be in range for his children:

> Sally Keeble to William Bounds – January 2, 1810
> William Keeble to Anne Malone – January 7, 1817

(3)   The secretiveness of the older generation regarding some clandestine event in William's earlier life, which showed a withholding of knowledge about where the event took place.

(4)   When William Keeble's son (Thomas), as Administrator of his mother's estate, went to Virginia in 1855 to determine what legacies were to come to the estate, he could find no record at all.

(5)   The strangest reason of all – when my wife and I were returning home from a visit to my parents in New York, we found lodging in West Virginia along the Ohio River. In looking in the phone book for Keebles, as I always do, I found Kibbles in Meigs County, Ohio. I called the residence and was greeted by interested kinfolk.

These folks were just as interested in finding their "roots" as we were. To make it even more curious, they could not find kinfolk earlier than the year 1800. Their tradition was that one Sophie Kibble had arrived in Ohio about 1800 on horseback with a young son, John. She died in 1840 at the age of 80 years, making her birth around 1760. Son John died July 30, 1875, aged 77 years, eleven months, and 25 days. This would make his birth around 1797.

Legend has it that Sophia was a withdrawn, taciturn woman who made no friends and lived entirely alone. Here we have the same situation with Sophia that we had with William. Their pasts held some deep dark secret. The dates of these two exact situations seem too alike to be mere coincidence. What kind of traumatic experience would elicit this kind of behavior – to never mention their lives before a certain date? We have located Sophia's signature on a document in Fauquier County, Virginia, in 1800 apparently just prior to her entering the new Ohio territory in 1800 at Marietta.

On December 17, 1799, just one month after the purchase and selling of the schooner boat, "The Greyhound," William Keeble married. He was 45 years old, and his bride was 15. I should state here that Wilson White, who sold The Greyhound schooner boat to William Keeble and William Sutton, later married William's wife's sister, Charlotte, and they moved to Tennessee a couple years later (1802).

According to newly discovered information from another branch of the family, William and his bride were cousins. They were married by the Reverend John Pickett, a Baptist Minister of the Gospel, in Fauquier County, Virginia.

According to one Mr. Eldon Irby of Abilene, Texas, his ancestors were John and Grace Anderson Keeble. They were married in Fauquier County and had the following children:

> James Stanford Keeble, born 1765
> John Keeble, born 1770
> Mary Keeble, born 1772
> Anderson Keeble, born 1775
> Suzannah Keeble, born 1780

Mr. Irby's chart relates that John Keeble, born 1770, married his cousin, Mary Keeble, on December 17, 1799. The chart also relates that Mary Keeble, born 1772, married her cousin, William Keeble, December 17, 1799, with the notation that each of the participants were cousins. I have no proof that his records are not correct; however, in the Fauquier County Marriage Bonds 1759-1854 and Returns 1785-1848 by John K. Gott, we find the following:

Page 116 – "Kibble, John and Mary, December 17, 1799 Bondsman
        (daughter of Richard)
        Kibble, William and Mary, December 19, 1799 Bondsman
        (none) John Pickett, Minister."

It would appear from this information that there was a double wedding on that day in December; however, John Kibble did not marry Mary Keeble, daughter of Richard. We have Richard Keeble's signature that his daughter has the right to marry William Keeble. It would appear to me that when William applied for a marriage license, John's name was substituted for his own and possibly not being able to read, he assumed he had the proper credentials to marry. Thus, a second marriage license had to be issued to William Keeble and Mary, daughter of Richard. To further prove the error, the marriage license of John and Mary was never returned to the courthouse for certification.

The license of William and Mary was duly signed by the minister and returned to the courthouse, was noted and certified. We have a photocopy of Reverend Pickett's ledger in which he enumerated all the marriages he had administered the rites of matrimony. William and Mary, daughter of Richard, are listed but no other Keebles. If there were two marriage rites performed that day, as Mr. Irby alleges, it was not a double wedding ceremony.

Richard Keeble's permissive statement for the marriage of Mary, page 31:

"This is to certify that I have consented for license to be granted in favor of William Kibbel to marry my daughter Mary Kibbel to the Clerk of Fauquier County." Richard Kibbel, December 16, 1799. Witnesses: Benjamin Morry and Isaac Palmer.

One would think that if the Reverend Pickett had married two couples that day, writing down William's wedding would have brought the other couple to mind and caused the second couple to be entered into his ledger.

As for extra proof that there was not a double marriage ceremony performed that December day in 1799, we have Declarations given by Mary herself and her friend Eleanor Harris in 1849, given in Blount County, Tennessee, where they both were living. Eleanor says that she attended the wedding and saw William and Mary united in marriage. Neither deposition mentioned a second couple being married that day.

In Mary's Declaration to obtain a widows pension, she relates that in the spring of 1800, she and William moved to Blount County, Tennessee, where they have resided ever after. There is no notation relative to their mode of transportation to the south. One would assume that it was by horse, oxen, and possibly ox-cart.

Fauquier County was inland where river transportation to the south would be impossible. They undoubtedly traveled west from Fauquier County some 20 or 25 miles to the present area of Front Royal, Virginia, where the Appalachian Mountain range begins and crossed through the gap at that

Harris

are held and firmly bound unto *James Monroe* Governor of Virginia, in the just

and full sum of one hundred and fifty dollars, to which payment well and truly to be made, to the said

Governor or his successors, we bind ourselves, our and each of us, heirs, executors and administrators,

jointly and severally, firmly by these presents. Sealed with our seals, and dated this *17* day of

December 1799

THE Condition of the above Obligation is such, that whereas there is a Marriage shortly intended to be

solemnized between *William Kibble* and ~~Benjamin~~ *Mary*

~~Harris~~ *Kibble*

now if there be no lawful cause to obstruct the said Marriage, then the above Obligation to be void,

otherwise to remain in full force and virtue.

Signed, sealed and delivered }
in the presence of }

William ✝ Kibble
mark

Whiting Diggs

Benjamin Harris

This is to satisfy that I have consented for
license to be granted In favour of William
Kibble to Marry My Daughter
Mary Kibble to the Clark of Fauquier
Court

Richard Kibble

Benjamin Darris

Isaac Bolmer

December 16 1799

A

Dec 19, 1796 John Smith & Elizabeth Dodd
Dec 26, 1796 Wm Doran & Mary Griffin
Dec 26, 1796 Doxty Armstrong & Judith Cruss
Do   Do Ambrosler & Elizabeth toʼkill

February 21, 1797 James Shalon & Martha Hand
April 9, 1797 Geo. Busley & Mary Jeffres
Sept 25, 1797 Edwin Porter & Polly Slausy
Sept Do Do Benjm. Hatcher & Mary McKenney
Dec 7, 1797 David Murphy & Lydia Dix

Mar 26, 1798 Samuel Pearce & Delia Darnall
Apr 21 Do Lewis Smith & Ruth Davis
Do Do Wm Bailly & Abigal Eaton
Sept 1 Do Saml. Armsted & Rebecca Fitch
Nov 29 Do Jesse Lowe & Jany Kemper
Dec 9, Do Sam Slaughter & Peggy Lamkin
Sept 16 Do James Smith & Chasey Spencer
Do Do Joshua Darnall & Jemima Slausy
25 Do John Sudduth & Nancy William
Apr 20 1799 Abraham Garner & Susanna titters
May 14 Do Harrisn Edge & Ann Ackermach
May 18 Do Geo Haines & Sealah tuthill
May 14 Do Ben James & Elizabeth
June 1 Do John Atwood & Lucy Robinson
Sept 29 Do Ephraim Epping & Jacitta Norman
Oct 17 Do Ezra Porter & Elizabeth Porter

Duty Jr 1799 Wm Kittle & Mary Kittle
Dec 22 Do this Anderson & Saly anderson
Dec 24 do David Darnall Selisby Bonton
Janu 1 Do Peter Kerns & Betsey Roby
Janu 2 Do Coman & Elizabeth Cotturtact
Do Do Lewis Smith & Elizabeth Clearwy
May 3, 1800 John Evans & Jany Wright
June 4 Do Eli Porter & Martha Dale
Do Do John Peack & Nancy Neale
Do Do James Senson & Judith Dale
Jay Do James Dale & Anne Clayhoole
Jany Do Blackaby & Elizabeth Palmer
Sept 13 Benjn. Duncan & Lettue Foley
Do Do Danl Dodd & Hannah Settle

To all whom it may concern of the County of Fauquier this to Certify that I have solemnized Matrimony between the persons whose names are under written. So wit:

Armand George and Elizabeth Turnbull
Nov 99. Edward Ballenger & Hannah Doe
Nov 99. James Stark & Eliz with
Duncan December 18, 99. Isaack Stout
and Lucina Read Jany 23 1800

John Hickerson

John Grimm to Catharine Simms

George Coots by to Elizabeth Peters.

<u>Nathaniel Grimes</u>

This is to certify that I Married
Nicholas Read and Peggy Duncan
of Fauquier county according
to law November 16th 1797.

                              William Read

Marriage —

This is to certify that I solemnize
matrimony between John Shuman
and Elizabeth Freeman of the
county of Fauquier January the
first 1797. John Nickerson

p 14

<u>Fauquier County</u>

Licenas confirmed by me John Robert X

October 30 1795. John Loman and Poly Atterburn
December 23 1795. Austin Waherny and Jemima ___
Do — Do — John Loikes and Elizabeth Wood
November 28 1795. Amos Snyder and Catharine Hall
Dec 2 9 1795. Moses Sygriss and Mary Wood
Dec 2 9 1795. David Comaga 8 Mary Wood
Do — James Bell 8 Aggy Grant
March 10 1796. Daniel Kempen 8 Nancy Kempen
Mar 2 1796. Wm Robinson 8 Nancy Fenner
June 3 1796. Sylvester Sullivan 8 Susan Robe
June 22 1796. Smith Farmer 8 Jane Ball
Jun 23 1796. Joel Pool and Jena Bird
Aug 1 — Peter Att and Lucy Att
Aug 22 1796. Samuel Porter 8 Potty
September 6 1796. John Loikes 8 Susanna Roper
September 8 1796. James Loikes 8 Dirksey Maury
Sept 14 1796. John Nilson 8 Feathy Loikes
Sept 26 1796. Henry Slaughter 8 Penny Taylor
Oct 8 1796. John Born 8 Judith Shurnett
Oct 20 1796. John Taylor 8 Peggy Arthas
Nov 23 1796. Joseph Grant 8 Elizabeth Taylor
Do Do 1796. James Barnett 8 Mary Barney
Dec — 1796. Wm Blabler 8 Ronel Garnes
Dec 22 1796. Henderlipps 8 Mary Palmer

point and turned left to head south on the Federal Road, which had been and was being used by the travelers from Pennsylvania and points north. William and Mary were on their way to the Old Southwest Territory. I am sure as they proceeded south, the road deteriorated into a narrow path and then to almost unblazed trail over tree stumps, creek beds, and rocky banks.

They would pass the Wilderness Road to the west blazed by Daniel Boone into Kentucky territory and finally perhaps were able to make log rafts to float on down to the Knoxville area in the new State of Tennessee, which was only four years old, having been admitted to the Union in 1796.

Mary was pregnant with Thomas as they made their way to their new environment. Thomas was born in Blount County, Tennessee, seven months after their marriage.

In 1800 Blount County was very primitive and unsettled. We do not know why William chose the area near present-day Walland to settle. Had he been to the area in the "lost" years of his life and had then sought out land that had not yet been legally available as it had belonged to the Cherokee Indian Nation? Another tradition comes to mind. When William came to the spot he desired to settle on, another person had "Squatters Rights" to that particular location. The recording of Land Deeds was not yet possible in the year 1800 in Blount County, and so one sat on the land awaiting the time when he could register a Deed. Keeble is said to have asked the original "Squatter" what he would take for his claim and was told "A bottle of whiskey." William was able to oblige the original claimant with the whiskey and assumed control over the acreage.

In the original Grant, a description of the boundaries of the property were listed, the date that the survey was made, and then the following, "To Have and to Hold the said parcel or tract of land with its appurtenances to the said William Keeble" (taken out of context).

The word appurtenances means any other improvement on the land being granted. The improvements usually meant a cabin or house, leanto, shack, or whatever the original "Squatter" had constructed to protect himself from the elements of the weather. However, it might mean cleared land, fruit orchard, a barn, any improvement from the basic natural condition of the land.

We must assume that the original settler on the Keeble land had a shelter of some kind in the winter and early spring of 1800.

Regarding Land Grants and Titlement of Land, in 1806 a law was passed by the State of Tennessee permitting land holders to title their land. Between 1794 and 1806, there was a dispute as to whether North Carolina, the State of Franklin (East Tennessee), or the State of Tennessee had the right to grant land in this part of East Tennessee. A requirement for the granting of land necessitated that the tenant live on the land for six months and improve it (Pre-emptive Rights). On January 7, 1807, William Keeble's land was surveyed. The plat was for 251-1/2 acres, 2 Rods, and 36 Perches. The land was on Little Ellejoy Creek, Blount County, Tennessee. The chain carriers were John Snider and William Taff . The assistants were James Garner, Wilson White, William Saffle, John Walker, Samuel Walker, and William Keeble. Wilson White was the husband of Mary Keeble's sister, Charlotte. William Keeble could not help in surveying his own land, and so we know there was another William Keeble in the community. Perhaps he was the son from the earlier family of William Keeble, our subject. On the 25th of May 1810, the Grant was approved by the State of Tennessee. John Snider, Samuel Walker, Robert Walker, and William Saffle all owned land adjoining Keeble's Grant, and thus these men made good chain carriers in defining the perimeter of their lands.

By the year 1817, according to William's Declaration, the first dwelling became entirely too small. Living in it were William, Mary, their eight children, the oldest 17, plus an orphan child. William Keeble bound to William Keeble, Sr., until he was 21 years.

William constructed a new residence on his property. In 1820 he declared that his new home was worth twenty dollars (with timber so readily available, most of the cost was labor).

At Knoxville on the twenty fifth day of May in the year of our Lord One
Thousand Eight Hundred and Ten and of American Independence the thirty
fourth.

By the Governor   Willie Blount
W. G. Blount, Secretary
Section Files North of Holston #141
State of Tennessee   No. 1357

To all to whom these presents shall come, Greetings:
Know ye that in pursance of an Act of the General Assembly dated on the
twenty third Day of November Eighteen Hundred and Nine hath granted by
the said State of Tennessee unto William Keeble a certain tract or parcel of
land containing two hundred and fifty one acres of land five Rood and thirty
six Perches within the Tract located for the use of Academies lying in the
County of Blount in the District South of French Broad and Houlston on
Little Ellejoy there being due and chargeable on said land the sum of two
hundred and fifty one dollars seventy two and one half cents with the
interest due thereon. Beginning at a beech and running with vacant land
and Henry Heinz, South forty one West twenty seven chains and five links
to a stake, then with John Snider South fifty three East and sixty two chains
and forty five links to a black oak, then with Samuel Walker South sixty six
East two chains and twenty eight links to a hickory, then with Robert
Walker North fifty East thirty four chains and thirty three links to a
sourwood, North sixty eight degrees thirty minutes, East nineteen chains
and thirty six links to a hickory sapling, North five degrees thirty minutes,
West eleven chains and fifteen links to a black oak, North fifty nine degrees
thirty minutes, East thirty six chains and thirty nine links to a stake, North
seventy five degrees thirty minutes with vacant land to a black oak and
North forty one, East nine chains to a stake, North seventy four, East fifteen
chains and forty one links to a poplar, North twenty nine, East sixteen
chains and thirty six links to a black oak, North sixty West with vacant land
and William Saffle thirty chains to a pine, North thirty eight, West sixty one
chains and forty one links to a black oak sapling, South forty West one
hundred thirty one chains to a stake, North forty two, West twenty three
chains and forty one links to the beginning. Surveyed, January, the
seventh Eighteen Hundred and Seven with appurtenances To have and to

hold the said tract or parcel of land with its appurtenances to the said William Keeble and his heirs and assigns forever. In Witness whereof Willie Blount Governor of the State of Tennessee hath here unto set his hand and cause the Great Seal of the said State to be affixed at Knoxville on the twenty fifth day of May Eighteen Hundred and Ten and of American Independence the Thirty Fourth. By the Governor   Willie Blount.

From our records, we know that William and his family had lived only four or five years in their new dwelling when the property was reclaimed by the State of Tennessee for nonpayment of an installment due September of 1821. Even as late as 1829, Keeble stated that he was occupying the land but had no title to it.

One must assume that since Keeble stayed on the land and was not evicted, the government finally relented and awarded him the land he had lived on for thirty years. I find no evidence of payment for the amount in arrears to return the title to him.

It is interesting to note that Wilson White, brother-in-law of William, applied for a Land Grant from the State of Tennessee in the same area as Keeble – "Lying in the County of Blount in the District South of the French Broad and Houlston Rivers on Little River one hundred and seventeen acres" for which he was charged one hundred and seventeen dollars.

White's land was surveyed March 12, 1807, and his document signed by Willie Blount, Territorial Government, on May 3, 1810.

William's land was surveyed January 7, 1807, and his document signed by William Blount on May 25, 1810.

In 1832 William made application to the State for a Land Grant of "The Property lying on the waters of Little River for forty-five acres."

This land was probably unclaimed land lying adjacent to Keeble and White's land. White himself would have had to declare "Squatters Rights" for his land when he and Charlotte Keeble White came to Tennessee after their marriage in Fauquier County in 1802.

Thus Wilson and Charlotte White had some sort of a cabin or lodging on their property. Family tradition revealed that Charlotte did not stay in "their" cabin in her last illness. The story related to me was that Charlotte, who was dying of T. B., moved to William and Mary's residence so that Mary could take care of her. In her last illness there in Mary and William's home, she looked up across the hill and said she wanted to be buried under a tall pine tree on the hillside – indeed where she is interred.

State of Tennessee   No. 17,772

To all to whom these presents shall come, Greetings:

Know ye that in consideration of an Entry made in the Entry Taker's Office of Blount County of No. 693 dated the 8th Day of March 1832 by William Keeble, there is GRANTED by the State of Tennessee unto the said William Keeble and his heirs a certain TRACT OF LAND containing forty five acres lying in the County aforesaid on the waters of Little River, beginning at a poplar corner to his occupancy thence south thirty nine, west twenty one chains to a black oak, south forty nine, east forty two chains to a stake, north thirty nine, east forty chains to a stake thence in part with Joseph P Ellidge, north forty eight, west sixty seven chains to a stake, Ellidge corner by a coal pit, south forty two, west nine chains to a stake in his own line, thence with the same south sixty, east twenty three chains to a black oak, south twenty nine, west sixteen and seven tenths chains to the beginning.

        Surveyed the 10th of April 1832

With its appurtenances to HAVE and to HOLD the SAID TRACT OR PARCEL OF LAND and its APPURTENANCES to the said William Keeble and his heirs forever MILITARY PENSIONS and BOUNTY LAND FILES – portions of the Pension W 1880 BL. Wt. 4-518 – 160-55 of William Keeble Revolutionary War Treasury Department of East Tennessee, Knoxville, January 1830.

I certify that a certain William Keeble, a citizen in the district of County South of the French Broad and Houlston Rivers was in possession of two hundred and fifty-one and a half acres of land laid out for academies under the donation of Congress by the Act of 1806 for the use of Academies in the State of Tennessee, and under a certain statute of the State of Tennessee for the collection of monies arising from said lands, that the above mentioned two hundred and fifty one and a half acres of land was sold on the 3rd or 4th of September 1821 for one installment due on said land and was purchased by the State of Tennessee for the sum of twenty-five dollars and twenty five cents . . . the said land was never redeemed under the provisions of said Act.

Millen Francis
Treasurer of East Tennessee

Keeble missed a payment on his property. It was repossessed by the State of Tennessee by paying him twenty five dollars and twenty five cents.

Keeble never moved off the land, and it apparently was subsequently given to him.

William Keeble died in possession of the original 251-1/2 acres of land plus the 45 acres granted in 1832. It was divided among his children following the death of his wife Mary in 1855. On this land, Mr. Keeble farmed with the assistance of his sons while they lived at home. His Will shows that at least one of his sons had use of a horse from the farm and another was to farm the land for a period of time, after which he would inherit a part of the land left to him.

In the Declarations to apply for a pension in the pages following his life's story, one can see the trials the family had with the loss of cattle and other farm animals. Because of the farm losses and loss of his sons' assistance, William in his old age sought a government pension to help the family survive. William claimed he was a cripple, but no further information regarding his physical appearance or his infirmities is revealed.

Mr. Keeble made his Will on December 27, 1834. In it he states that he is very ill and knows he is about to die. Certainly his mind was still coherent, but we do not know the nature of his final illness. He did succumb on December 30, 1834, at the age of 79 years, presumably at his home. His Will had been dictated just three days prior to his death.

Mr. Keeble was buried on his own property, and his grave is in close proximity to the grave of Charlotte Keeble White, sister of Mary. William's grave has been honored by the Daughters of the American Revolution, giving their accreditation to the final resting place of a Revolutionary War Veteran (DAR #547683). Adjacent to the Keeble graveyard lies the lands of William Keeble's Land Grant.

Still standing near the scene of the original homeplace, two chimneys remain sentinels of a bygone era. It is quite possible that one of the chimneys was the site of Sarah's cabin. The other is probably the chimney to the smokehouse for the curing of hams and the storage of foodstuffs. A free-flowing stream is in close proximity to where the cabin stood. I do not know if the "coal pit" described as being a part of the 45-acre deed is still in evidence.

As mentioned before, it was only through the Declarations of William and Mary Keeble in their effort to obtain pensions from the government that we were able to relate with some degree of accuracy their lives and that of their progeny.

In conclusion of this biography, it seems fitting to add the remark of Mr. W. H. Keeble, great grandson of William, written in a letter to me at least fifty years ago. "In my lifetime I have known a great many Keebles - few aspired to greatness, the remainder were a pleasant lot, industrious and well behaved. I knew of no horse thieves or criminals among them." – AWD

WILL OF WILLIAM KEEBLE
Will Book #1 Blount County, Tennessee

In the name of God, Amen. I, William Keeble of the County of Blount, State of Tennessee being very sick and knowing it is appointed for all men once to die though of sound mind and disposing memory, for which I desire to thank God, and being desirous to dispose of all that worldly substance it hath pleased God to bless me with, do institute, make and appoint this my last Will and Testament in words and form following:

First, it is my will that after my death my body shall be buried in a decent Christian manner.

Second, it is my will that all my just and lawful debts shall be paid.

Third, it is my will that my wife Polly Keeble shall have and possess all that I possess at the time, with the condition with my son, Walter is to have the 75 acres of land which I lately conveyed to him by gift and the colt he is to have, but said Walter is to stay on the farm and take care of his mother for two years after my death and then have possession of the above named articles. The yoke of oxen also is to be Walters but has to remain on the farm and be subject to the use of the farm for four years after my death.

Fourth, it is my will that my son John Keeble and daughter Sally Keeble, my son William Keeble and my daughter Nancy Keeble or her heirs shall have one dollar each and no more.

Fifth, it is my will that the property that I now leave with my present wife at her death shall be equally divided amongst her children.

Sixth, information says to me that there is a legacy yet remaining from my fathers' and mothers' estate – should it ever be yet obtained it is my will that it shall be equally divided amongst all my lawfully born children.

Seventh, it is my will that the legacy which may yet be obtained from my present wifes' connections when received shall be equally divided amongst her own children.

Eight, it is my will that my daughter Polly B. Keeble, Sherlotte W. Keeble and Jane H. Keeble as they come of age shall be furnished with a bed containing 25 lbs. of good feathers and other furniture for said bed in properties.

Ninth, it is my will that my executors in the space of seven months after my death take the horse that Thomas Keeble now has in possession and make sale of said horse in whatever way they may think most advantageous and divide the proceeds amongst my three daughters.

Tenth, it is my will at the death of my wife my black woman Sarah shall have the privilege of making choice of a home to live at. It is my will that my wife Polly Keeble shall execute this my last will.

Witnessed the 27th of December 1834.

William (X) Keeble

Proven in Open Court that William Keeble died on December 30, 1834, that he was a Revolutionary War Soldier and left a widow Mary Keeble asking for a pension.

Court Minutes Vol 5 Pg. 56   March 26, 1835

Following are William Keeble's Declarations to the United States Government in order to receive a pension and other benefits.

State of Tennessee }   1818
Blount County Viz: }

Be it remembered that this day came William Keeble, citizen and resident of and in the said County who says he is and appears to be upwards of sixty three years of age, before me James Turk presiding Justice of the Court of Pleas and Quarter Sessions in and for the said County (which Court is a Court of Record) and the said William Keeble being duly sworn according to the law, doeth on his oath make the following declaration in order to obtain the benefits of a late Act of Congress passed the 18th day of March, 1818 entitled (An Act to provide for certain persons engaged in the land, and naval service of the United States in the Revolutionary War) to wit: that he, the said William Keeble did enlist in Fauquier County in the State of Virginia in the Company of Captain James Scott of the Regiment commanded by Colonels Toliver and Stephens and Major Thomas Marshall for the term of one year during which time he served as a Private Soldier, and was in the battle known by the name of The Battle of the Long Bridge in the State of Virginia and at the expiration of said term of one year he was honorably discharged.

That in the Month of August, 1777, the said William Keeble again enlisted from the County and State last aforesaid, in Captain Elias Edmonds Company of Artillery of Colonel Thomas Marshall's Regiment of the Virginia line in which regiment he served three years as a bombardier and was again honorably discharged in Richmond, Virginia, on the 22nd of August, 1780 and in the year 1781 was in the Militia Service at the Siege of York and capture of Lord Cornwallis, and late in the fall of the same year, just before Christmas, was well as this deponent now recollects, he enlisted in Captain Beverly Ray's Company in the Regiment commanded by Major Finley and Colonel Posey and marched to the South and was in the battle at the defeat of Old King Sago, the Indian Chief, about four miles south above Savannah in the State of Georgia besides some other skirmishes and late in the Fall 1782 was marched back to Cumberland Old Courthouse in the State of Virginia and again honorably discharged, all of which said the discharges are now lost or so mislaid that this deponent cannot find them, nor does he know of any other or better evidence of the facts above stated than the deposition of Mr. James Kennard herewith accompanying, that he claims no pensions from the United States or any of them, otherwise than under the late Act of Congress above mentioned, and that from his reduced circumstances in life he needs the assistance of his country for support. Sworn to and subscribed before me the 6th day of June 1818.

James Turk

His
William (X) Keeble
Mark

State of Tennessee }   1818
Blount County Viz: }

     Be it remembered that this day came Mr. James Kennard a respectable citizen of and in said county, before me thru said James Turk presiding Justice of the Court, and being duly sworn deposeth and saith that he has long been acquainted with the above named William Keeble, that he served with him in Captain Edmonds Company of Colonel Marshall's Regiment for the term of three years and was in the same mess with him during the said term of his second enlistment and service, and that from his knowledge of the other facts and of the circumstances and from his knowledge of the said William as to his character for veracity, he, this deponent has no doubt but that the facts as above stated by him the said William are true.

Sworn to and Subscribed before me   His
the 6th day of June, 1818.   James (X) Kennard
                                      Mark

State of Tennessee }   1818
Blount County Viz: }

I, the above mentioned, James Turk Presiding Justice of the Court of Pleas and Quarter Sessions in and for the said County do hereby certify, that it appears to my satisfaction that the said William Keeble did serve in the Revolutionary War against the common enemy as by him above stated, and do transmit the proceedings and testimony had and taken thereon, before me to the Secretary for the Department of War of the United States according to the Act of Congress in that case made and provided.

Given under my hand at Maryville in   James Turk
The County aforesaid this 6th day of June, 1818.

State of Tennessee ⎬   June 1829
Blount County Viz: ⎬

June Session of the County Court for the County and State aforesaid know this the 23rd day of June 1829.

Personally appeared in open Court being a Court of Record for the County and State aforesaid by the Laws of this State, William Keeble, resident in the said County aged about 75 years. Who being first fully sworn according to law doth on his oath make the following declaration in order to obtain the provisions made by the Act of Congress on the 18th of March 1818 and first of May 1820 that he the said William Keeble enlisted in August in the year 1777 for a term of three years in the State of Virginia in the Company of Artillery commanded by Captain Lias Edmons Regiment of Artillery commanded by Colonel Thomas Marshel – in the Line of the State of Virginia on the Continental Establishment; that he continued to serve said corpse until the twenty-second of August, 1780 when he was discharged from the service at Richmond, in the State of Virginia and that he enlisted as he believes in the year 1781 in the Company commanded by Captain Beverly Ray, Regiment commanded by Colonel Posey – in the Line of the State of Virginia, on the Continental Establishment – that he continued to serve said corps until the Army was discharged in 1782; that he hereby relinquishes every claim whatever to a pension except the present. That his name is not enrolled in any state in the United States and that the following are his reasons for not making earlier application for a pension: Is that here to fore he has been able to support himself by the assistance of his children who has lately left him; and another reason is that he has been an occupant on the land generally known by the land lying south of French-Broad and Holston Rivers, and as he was unable to pay the installments the land was sold to pay the installments: and that he has become very infirm and scarcely able to do any work whatever as he is a cripple. And in pursuance of the Act of the 1st May 1820, I do solemnly swear that I was a resident citizen of the United States on the 18th of March 1818 and that I have not since that time by gift sale or in any manner disposed of my property, or any part there of, with intent thereby to so diminish it as to bring myself within the provisions of an Act of Congress entitled "an act to provide for certain persons engaged in the land and naval service of the United States in the Revolutionary War" passed on the 18th day of March, 1818 and that I have not, nor has any person in trust for me any securities, contracts or debts due to me nor have I any income other than what is contained in the schedule here unto annexed and by me subscribed. That on the 18th of March 1818 I had the following articles of property to wit: Two-hundred fifty (250) Acres of land the value not known had not a title was only an occupant. Two horses each worth about $20.00, four head of sheep worth $1.00 each – the above is all the property I had at the time above mentioned except some household furniture, some bedding and some wearing clothes. The 250 acres of land was sold by the Treasurer of East Tennessee to pay the installments due upon it, which was bought by said Treasurer for the use of the State aforesaid: One of the above named horses I sold to Nicholas Norton and appropriated the money to the use of my family; all four of the above named sheep died.

The following is a complete schedule of the property I have at this time, to wit: One negro woman supposed to be 60 years old worth $50.00. One sorrel horse 14 years old worth $20.00. One horse 12 years old worth $20.00, one mare and colt worth $25.00, three milk cows worth $18.00, seven head of small cattle worth $17.00, 21 hogs worth $21.00, two sheep worth $2.50, one cupboard and furniture worth $6.00, one chest worth $2.50; kitchen furniture worth $7.00, farming utensils worth $6.00, one iron wedge worth $37.00, one drawing knife worth $37.00. I am indebted $12.00, $4.00 are owing me, three of which are insolvent. The above is all the property I own in the world except my bedding and wearing clothes. The declarant is a farmer but is unable to do anything at farming or anything else in consequence of his infirmity and crippled situation. The following are the names of declarants children that are with him: Rebecca Keeble age 19 years, Richard Keeble aged about 18 years, Walter Keeble aged 13 years, and very sickly, Polly Keeble aged 10 years, Charlotte Keeble aged about five years, Jane about 4 years. Declarants wife is sickly and unable to assist in making support for the family. Declarant is so old and infirm that it is impossible for him to get any account of the sale of the land he lives on, he therefore prays that the Secretary of War will give him that which he is honestly entitled to.

Sworn to and subscribed in open Court   His
The 23rd day of April, 1829, Jac. Foute Clk.   William (X) Keeble
By his Deputy D. D. Foute   Mark

State of Tennessee }   1829
Blount County Viz: }

December Sessions of the County Court for the County and State aforesaid for the year 1829.

On this 29th day of December, 1829 personally appeared in open court, it being a Court of Record for the County and State aforesaid by the laws of this State William Keeble a resident in said county aged about 75 years who being first duly sworn according to law, doth on his oath make the following declaration in order to obtain the provision made by the Act of Congress on the 18 March, 1818 and the 1st of May 1820 that he the said William Keeble enlisted in August in the year 1777 for the term of three years in the State of Virginia in the Company of Artillery commanded by Captain Lias Edmons Regiment of Artillery commanded by Colonel Thomas Marshall in the Line of the State of Virginia on the Continental Establishment and that he continued to serve said corpse until the 22nd of August 1780 when he was discharged from the service in Richmond in the State of Virginia, and that he enlisted as he believes in the year 1781 in the Company commanded by Captain Beverly Ray, the Regiment commanded by Colonel Posey in the Line of the State of Virginia on the Continental Establishment, and that he continued to serve said corpse until the army was discharged in 1782.

That he hereby relinquishes every claim whatever to a pension except the present; that his name is not enrolled in any State in the United States and that the following are his reasons for not making earlier application for the pension: the first reason he did not make an earlier application for a pension is that here to fore he has been able to support himself by the assistance of his children who have lately left him. The second reason is that he has been an occupant on the land known by the land lying south of the French Broad and Houlston Rivers and as he was unable to pay the installments on the 3rd or 4th day of September 1821 the land was sold by the Treasurer of East Tennessee to pay said installments and that he has become very infirm and scarcely able to do any work whatsoever as he is a cripple. And in pursuance of the Act of May 1820 I do solemnly swear that I was a resident citizen of the United States on the 18th day of March 1818 and I have not since that time by gift, sale or in any manner disposed of my property or any part thereof with intent thereby to so diminish it as to bring myself within the provisions of the Act of Congress entitled an Act to provide for certain persons engaged in the Land and Naval Service of the United States in the Revolutionary War, passed on the

18th of March 1818, and that I have not now any person in trust for me any property or securities, contract, or debts due to me nor have I any income other than what is contained in the schedule here unto annexed and by me subscribed. That on the 18th day of March 1818 I had the following articles of property to wit: 251-1/2 acres of land, value not known, had no title was only an occupant, two horses worth about $20.00, four head of sheep worth $1.00 each. The above is all the property I had at the time above mentioned except some household furniture, some bedding and some wearing clothes. The 251-1/2 acres of land was sold by the Treasurer of East Tennessee to pay the installments, and purchased by said Treasurer for the use of the State aforesaid and has never been redeemed. The above named horses I sold to Nicholas Norton and appropriated the money for the use of my family; all four of the above named sheep died. The following is a complete schedule of the property I have at this time to wit: One negro woman supposed to be 60 years old worth $50.00, three head of horses worth $25.00, one horse died the last of July 1829, six head of cattle worth $25.00, two head of cattle died sometime in the first of August, 1829, three head of sheep worth $3.00, fourteen head of hogs worth $8.50, three beds and furniture worth $30.00, farming utensils $8.00, kitchen furniture, one chest, one cupboard worth $12.00. I killed two small steers for the use of my family in the Fall of 1829, seven hogs died sometime in August 1829, one bed, my daughter married and took it away with her. Declarant is indebted about $23.00 to different persons for the support of his family.

The above is all the property I own in the world. The declarant is a farmer by occupation but is unable to do anything at farming or anything else in consequence of his infirmity and crippled situation.

The following are the names of declarants children that are with him: Richard Keeble aged about 18 years, Walter Keeble aged about 13, very sickly has a wen on his breast, Polly Keeble aged about 10 years. Charlotte Keeble aged about 5 years, and Jane Keeble aged 4 years. Declarants wife is very sickly and unable to assist in making support for the family. The Certificate of the Treasurer of East Tennessee showing the disposition of his land is herewith transmitted to the Department of War. He therefore prays the Secretary of War will give him that which he is entitled to.

His
William (X) Keeble
Mark

Sworn and subscribed in Open Court 29th December 1829
Jac. F. Foute, Clerk
By his Deputy D. D. Foute

I Jacob F. Foute Clerk of the Court of Pleas and Quarter Sessions for the County of Blount and State of Tennessee do hereby certify that it appears to the satisfaction of the Court that the said William Keeble did serve in the Revolutionary War as stated in the preceeding declaration against the common enemy for the term of nine months under one engagement on the Continental Establishment.

3—525

Ew

W. 1880.

DEPARTMENT OF THE INTERIOR,

BUREAU OF PENSIONS.

Washington, D. C., *Sept 12*, 1922

Will E. Parham,
Maryville, Tenn.

Sir:—

In reply to your request of *Aug. 18*, for the history of *William Keeble*, a soldier of the Revolutionary War, the following is taken from the *Soldier's & Widow's* claim for pension.

DATES OF ENLISTMENT OR APPOINTMENT.	LENGTH OF SERVICE.	RANK.	OFFICERS UNDER WHOM SERVICE WAS RENDERED.		STATE.
			CAPTAIN.	COLONEL.	
✓	1 year	Pvt	James Scott	Toliver Stephens	Va.
Aug. 1777	3 years	Bombardier.	Elias Edmunds	Thomas Marshall	
1781	1 year	Pvt	Beverly Ray	Posey	

Battles engaged in, *Long Bridge; Siege of York; & with Indians*

Residence of soldier at enlistment, *Enlisted in Fauquier Co., Va*

Date of application for pension, *June 6, 1818. His claim was allowed at 6*

Residence at date of application, *Blount Co., Tenn.*

Age at date of application, *63 years, died Dec. 30, 1834 in Blount Co., Tenn.*

Remarks: _____

Respectfully,

Washington Gardner

, Commissioner.

A

WILLIAM KEEBLE

WIFE

MARY KEEBLE KEEBLE

THE

HOLY BIBLE.

CONTAINING

THE OLD AND NEW TESTAMENTS:

TRANSLATED OUT OF

THE ORIGINAL TONGUES,

AND WITH THE

FORMER TRANSLATIONS DILIGENTLY COMPARED AND
REVISED.

STEREOTYPE EDITION.

NEW-YORK:
STEREOTYPED BY L. CHANDLER,
FOR THE AMERICAN BIBLE SOCIETY.
1830.

[Nonpareil 18mo.]

Mary Raeble
her Book 1895

1st Return
August

Elizabeth C.
Dunlap
was born Oct. 16
1893

A

William Kirtle Born
May 23rd 1735

Mary Kirtle Born July
29th 1884

Horno Kirtle Born July
31st 1800

Samuel Kirtle Born
March 2nd 1802

Hannah Stamps Kirtle
Born March 22nd 1805

Monty Kirtle Born
July 3rd 1807

Rebecca Kirtle Born
January 9th 1811

Richard Kirtle Born
January 19th 1811

Harriet Kirtle Born
July 3rd 1813

J B P Dunlap and
Wellary Holloway
married Sept 14 1892

E P Dunlap was born
Apr 22, 1868

Hallie A. adastons
Oct 28, 1871

Elizabeth G. Dunlap
was born Oct 1 1893

Maud Estell Dunlap
was born Sept 21, 1895

Anna P Dunlap
Died July 16 1895

Clark Estell Dunlap
died

MARY KEEBLE KEEBLE

Mary Keeble was born on Leap Year Day – February 29, 1784, the daughter of Richard Keeble and Hannah Stamps Keeble. Her birth date is recorded in her Bible, which is shown on the following pages. Since her legal documents throughout her life were signed with an "X," we must assume that she could not write.

Her mother's family had been in Fauquier County, Virginia, for a number of years. One of Mary's great-grandfathers on the distaff side was Thomas Stamps, Sr., who is said to have been born in Lancaster County, Virginia, about the year 1700. He died in Fauquier County, and his Will was probated there in May of 1763. In his Will he stated: "To granddaughter, Hannah Stamps, daughter of my son Thomas, Dec'd. 15 lbs. when she arrives at age 18."

The wife of Thomas Stamps, Sr., was Mary Rose, daughter of John and Mary Rose of Northumberland County, Virginia. Mary's grandfather on the distaff side was Thomas Stamps, Jr., who, as mentioned above, died before his father. Thomas, Jr., married Lydia, daughter of Joseph and Lydia Duncan. The Duncan, Rose, and Stamps family lines have been traced back several generations.

Thomas Stamps, Jr., and Lydia Duncan Stamps had two daughters, Molly and Hannah Stamps, Hannah being the mother of Mary Keeble, our subject. Joseph Duncan, in his Will of February 13, 1792, lists his wife Lydia and a daughter, Lydia O'Bannon, wife of John O'Bannon, his son-in-law. Apparently after the death of Thomas Stamps, Jr., his widow, Lydia, married John O'Bannon, dropping the Stamps name.

We have a document on the following page in which Lydia O'Bannon makes a gift to her daughter, Hannah Stamps, the mother of Mary, a negro slave, Benjamin, sixteen years of age.

Gift of a Slave From Mary Keeble's Grandmother to Her Mother Hannah
Deed Book #17, Pg. 135, August 1807

"Know all men by these presents that I, Lydda O'Bannon of the County of Fauquier and State of Virginia, for and in Consideration of the Natural love and affection which I bear to my Daughter Hannah Keeble of the County and State aforesaid, as well as for the further consideration of one Dollar to me in hand paid by the said Hannah Keeble at or before unsealing and delivering of these presents the Receipt thereof is hereby acknowledged have given and granted by these presents do give and grant unto the said Hannah Keeble, her heirs, Executors, Administrators and Assigns one negro Boy Named Benjamin about sixteen years of age, To have and to hold the said Negro unto her the said Hannah Keeble forever and the said Lydda O'Bannon for Herself, her Heirs, Executors, Administrators, give said Negro unto the said Hannah Keeble, her Heirs, Executors, Administrators and assigns against the Claim of her the said Lydda Her Heirs, Executors, Administrators and against the Claim of all and every person or persons whatever shall and will warrant and forever defend by these presents in witnessing where of I have hereunto set my Hand and affixed my seal this 29th day of August one thousand Eight Hundred and Seven."

Signed and Sealed
In the presence of us
Wm. <u>Howe</u>?
&
Edward Burgess
John Burgess

Her
Lydda (X) O'Bannon
Mark

At a Court held for Fauquier County the 22nd day of February 1808 this Deed of Gift was proved to be the act of love of the said Lydda O'Bannon by the oaths of Edward Burgess and John Burgess witnesses there – to and accent to be recorded.

Feliz H. R. _____ &c.

You will notice that the gift of the negro slave, Ben, was legalized in August 1807.

The children of Richard Keeble and Hannah Stamps Keeble were:

- Mary Keeble, who married William Keeble December 17, 1799, and who is one of the subjects of this book.
- Fanny Keeble, who married Humphrey Davis in Fauquier County, Virginia, on February 20, 1802. Fanny died (date unknown) prior to her father's death in 1811. I do not know if she had descendants.
- Charlotte Keeble, who married Wilson White on September 25, 1802, in Fauquier County, Virginia. Charlotte also died prior to her father's death in 1811. They had a daughter Eliza White. Charlotte is buried in the Keeble Cemetery, Blount County, Tennessee.
- Charles G. Keeble married Nancy Selman in Fauquier County, Virginia, on January 9, 1816. He died in Paducah, Kentucky, in 1856. I do not know if they had any heirs.
- Thompson Keeble married Sarah Ford on February 3, 1817, in Fauquier County, Virginia. They were living in Warren County, Virginia, in 1850. Warren County is adjacent to Fauquier County to the west. I do not know if they had children.
- Harriett Keeble did not marry. In Will Book #14, November 21, 1816, to June 1836 in Fauquier County, we find the following: "Harriett Keeble- To my loving Mother Hannah Keeble the residue of my Rights of the Estate of my Father, Richard Keeble, Dec'd. and at her death to be equally divided between my sister, Mary Keeble and brothers Thompson and Charles G. Keeble and my niece, Eliza White."

This is our only mention of a daughter of Charlotte and Wilson White, and we do not know if she lived to womanhood. It was Charlotte, above, who was reported to have died of tuberculosis.

It is apparent from Richard's treatment of both William Keeble and Wilson White in his Will that he was unhappy with them. Was it Richard's feeling as a result of the men taking his daughters so far from home or was he at odds with the idea of grown men marrying his teenage daughters and one of them, Mary, being pregnant at age fifteen (William was 44)? At this time, we do not know but what Richard and William were brothers and William was marrying his niece.

LAST WILL AND TESTAMENT OF RICHARD KEEBLE OF VIRGINIA

Dated: 18 October 1811

(Father of Mary Keeble)

I, Richard Keeble, in the County of Fauquier, in the Commonwealth of Virginia, being of sound mind, considering the certainty of death and the uncertainty of when it may happen, have determined to make this (my last will and testament), in the manner following: that is to say I give and bequeath to my dearly beloved wife, Hannah Keeble, a negro fellow by the name of (Ben), during her widowhood. In case she should marry, the said (Ben) is to be taken and equally divided between my three children (Viz) Thompson Keeble, Charles Keeble and Harriet Keeble. Or at any rate, marry or not, at her expiration the said (Ben) to be equally divided between the above mentioned children.

I also give to my wife one featherbed and furniture during her natural life, then to the three children in manner aforesaid. I also give her all my livestock of every denomination, also the necessary utensils about my house such as tables, chests, chairs, pewter, etc. and at her death return in like manner as above. Item: I give and bequeath to my above named three children, that is to say Thompson, Charles and Harriet, the residue of my negroes, namely, Fanny, Ephraim, Thornton, and Susannah, and their increase during their natural lives, after my decease to be equally divided between them.

These legatees are to make no division until my debts are all paid of that which should come against my estate with interest from the time of my death, my funeral expenses, etc.

Item: I give and bequeath to William Keeble, in the Tennessee State, who married my daughter Molly and her heirs five shillings sterling.

Item: I give and bequeath to Wilson White, of the Tennessee State, who married my daughter Sharlotte, deceased, and her heirs five shillings sterling.

Item: I give and bequeath to Humphrey Davis, who married my daughter Fanny, deceased, five shillings sterling.

It is my will and desire that the three above named, should be cut off and receive no more out of my estate than the sum mentioned.

In witness where of I have hereunto set my hand and seal this the eighteenth of October in the year of our Lord Eighteen Hundred and Eleven.

Signed, sealed, and declared by the said Richard Keeble as his last will and testament, in the presence of Zachariah Silman, Allison Ford, and Chandler Ford.

Note: At a court held in Fauquier County on the 28th day of April, 1812 this will and testament of Richard Keeble, deceased, was in open court approved by the oaths of Allison Ford, and Chandler Ford, Subscribing Witnesses thereto and ordered to be recorded.

A Copy Teste   A. J. Marshall   C.C.

The original copy of this Will was given to me by J. H. Farmer at his daughter's home (Mrs. Clemmie Dunlap). Mr. Farmer stated that he was present when the old Keeble home was torn down. A whole passel of papers were thrown out of the loft and into the mud. Mr. Farmer stated that this paper looked important so he picked it up and kept it.

(Mr. Farmer referred to the old Thomas Keeble home when it was torn down.)

Hannah's husband, Richard, in his Will of 1811, left a Negro slave named Ben to his widow if she not marry; if she marries, Ben is to be equally divided between Richard's three children, namely Thompson, Charles G., and Harriett. Thus Ben, the slave given to Hannah by her mother in 1807, became the property of her husband through marriage and he in turn Wills Ben to Hannah if she does not marry again. Richard mentions the names of his other slaves in his Will so that we know slave Ben was the same person in each instance.

Here in Blount County, Tennessee, William and Mary Keeble resided as of the year 1800 and Mary gave birth to eleven children. The 1840 Census for Blount County lists Mary as head of the household, as William had died in 1834. The Census lists her as between 40 and 50 years of age. She was in fact 55 years at the time. From the 1880 Census for Blount County, in which the place of birth is requested for the parents of each citizen, William and Mary's children (Hannah Dunlap, Jane, and Richard Keeble) all state that their mother was born in Virginia. In the 1850 Census when Mary was interviewed by the Census Taker, he reported Mary was born in North Carolina. Her age was given correctly and her widowhood confirmed. Living with her were two children, John (age 25) and Mary (age 18). I have no knowledge as to who these young people belonged.

I have attempted to give insight into the lives of each of William and Mary's children as related to me by their descendants. I will leave it to others to write biographies of the ancestors of their respective lines. Mary died June 15, 1855, about age 70, and she is buried near her husband and sister, Charlotte. Many other family members do not have grave markers denoting their final resting places. They all repose on land which was a part of William Keeble's land grant and which was sold by the children after the death of their mother. At a later date, the cemetery was repurchased by family members to protect the hallowed ground that their loved ones were interred upon.

One will note in reading the tombstone epitaph on Mary Keeble's grave that her name is inscribed there as MARY WHITE KEEBLE. As we have stated before, Mary was a KEEBLE prior to her marriage. The gravestone should read MARY KEEBLE KEEBLE. Mr. Pleasant Keeble, who was responsible for having the markers fashioned and placed on the graves of William Keeble and his family in the Keeble Church graveyard, was mistaken when he had Mary's inscription inscribed.

In a letter written to the author by Pleasant Keeble's son, William H. Keeble, he states, "I am wholly unable to account for my father's idea as to who William Keeble's second (wife) was; that is as to her background. He apparently always thought that her name was simply Mary White. If he ever knew that her name was Mary Keeble, he never mentioned it to me. But I have often heard him criticize himself severely for giving so little heed, when he was a youngster, to the great store of family history which his father, Manly Keeble possessed." (Page #4 of a letter written March 29, 1958.

It is my theory that Pleasant knew that Mary's sister, Charlotte, was the first person buried in the Keeble Graveyard. He perhaps did not know that Charlotte had been married to Wilson White and assumed that the family name of the two women was White. Charlotte had died prior to her father's death (Richard Keeble), that fact being recorded in Richard Keeble's Will written in 1811. Pleasant Keeble was not born until 1845, and it is my thought that he didn't have the tombstones erected until he was in mid-life, perhaps 1885-1895 or later.

It would appear that Wilson White and Eliza White, their daughter, had either died or removed from the area. Perhaps tuberculosis had ravaged the family as it had the mother. We just do not know. Thus quite possibly, Pleasant did not know or realize at that late date that Charlotte had been a Keeble, and he assumed White was Charlotte and Mary's family name. I can think of no other reason for Mr. Pleasant Keeble's error in Mary's tombstone epitaph.

Declaration in order to obtain benefit of the Act of Congress on the 29th of July 1848

State of Tennessee
County of Blount Viz:

On this fifth day of November one thousand eight hundred and forty nine personally appeared before the county court of Blount County, in the State of Tennessee aforesaid, being a court of record, Mary Keeble, a resident of said county and state aged sixty five years in February last, now being duly sworn according to law, doeth on her oath make the following declaration, in order to obtain the benefit of the provisions of the Act of Congress, made and approved the 29th of July 1848 entitled: "An Act of relief of certain surviving widows of officers and soldiers of the Revolutionary Army." That she is the widow of William Keeble, who was a private soldier in the army of the revolution: that she is wholly indebted to information from her husband, the said William Keeble and others, who served with him, for all the knowledge she possesses of his services and enlistment in the Revolutionary War. Her husband informed her that he enlisted in Fauquier County in the State of Virginia shortly, as well as she remembers, after the commencement of said war, under Captain Elias Edmonds. She thinks he informed her he was in the service about seven years, that he was at sometime during the service stationed for about two years at Williamsburg in the State of either Maryland or Virginia, that he was at Yorktown at the Seige, and was present at the surrender of Cornwallis that at sometime during the war he had served under Captain Boyles. She has been acquainted with and informed by, Andrew Smith and James Kanard she well remembers, was witness for her said husband to prove his service in said war, when he applied for a pension under the Act of Congress of the 18th of March 1818 from whose evidence and perhaps of others he was allowed a pension in 1819. Some few years afterwards, her husband was called in by Andrew Smith as a witness for him to prove his services in the said war, in an application or to accompany a declaration made of which applications, are, as she presumes, on file in the pension office.

Her husband was allowed to draw a pension, under the Act of Congress of the 18th of March 1818 for some 2-3 years discontinued or suspended for some years, and again revived from the 3rd of February 1830, agreeable to the Act of Congress of the 1st of March 1823 for some two or three years. When his pension was discontinued or suspended for some years, and again revived from the 3rd of February 1830, agreeable to the Act of

Congress of the first of March 1823 as appears from the accompanying letter, from the Commissioner of Pensions of the 18th of March 1830, appended to this declaration. This is the only evidence of record in her power or possession, so far as she knows, to present before the Department as proof of her said husbands services; To which she appends an affidavit, of her said husband, found after his death, among his papers. Which to and examining his claim: To the paper of which, and the evidence there in contained, she refers the Commissioner for satisfactory proof of her husbands services. That she can produce (Kanard and Smith now being dead) no other proof, of which she is now informed of her said husbands services. She further declares that she was married to the said William Keeble on the 17th day of December 1799 in Fauquier County, in the State of Virginia. That she removed with her husband, the said William Keeble, shortly there after from the State of Virginia in the winter or spring of 1800 to Little River in Blount County, Tennessee, in the vicinity of which place she has ever since resided and now resides. That her said husband died at his residence in said County of Blount on the 30th day of December 1834. That she was not married to him prior to his leaving the service but that their marriage took place previous to the second day of January 1800 Viz: at the time above stated. She further swears she is still a widow and that she has never been married to any other man; and that she never before made an application for a pension of any kind except arrears at the time of his death of her said deceased husband. That she was married on the said 17th day of December 1799 by John Pickett of the Baptist Order or Church, a clergyman and minister of the gospel in Fauquier County in the State of Virginia as before stated, that this minister gave her a certificate of her said marriage and advised her that as she was very young to take care of it, that it might be of use to her, but not having appreciated his advice she has long since lost or mislaid the certificate and cannot now produce it to present with her declaration. That she has no family record of her said marriage nor is it within her power to produce any other record there of to her knowledge nor any other evidence there of except such as is hereby subjoined, and therewith presented before the Honorable Commissioner of Pensions.

Sworn and Subscribed in open court this 5th of November 1849 by the above named Mary Keeble.

Robert A. Tedford
Mary Keeble

Personally appeared John Henry aged sixty years and Samuel Henry aged 72 years, and Adam Haun a Justice of the county, before the County Court of Blount County being a court of record of said county in the State of Tennessee and made oath in due form of law that they, and each of them, are and have been since the winter or spring of 1800 personally acquainted with Mary Keeble, whose name is subscribed to the foregoing declaration, at which time she removed with her husband, William Keeble from, as affiants understood and believed, some part of Virginia, to their immediate neighborhood in said County of Blount on Little River in which vicinity and within three miles of each of them she and her said husband resided until the time of his death about the last of December eighteen hundred and thirty four where she has since resided, and now resides.

She was then represented to be and has ever since been reputed to be the true and lawful wife of him the said William Keeble, and was so acknowledged and treated by him, until his death, which fact they confidentially believe. That they believe she is, when in oath entitled to implicit credit, that her husband, the said William Keeble, many years since, drew a pension from the government, which was for some reason, for a time discontinued or suspended and again allowed before his death – they are unable to give dates – they further state, that the said William Keeble, departed this life about the last of December 1834 as aforesaid, at his residence in their said vicinity in Blount County, Tennessee, leaving the above named declarant, his widow and relict. That she has been since his death, and is now, his widow, and as such they named Mary Keeble, and believe the statements there in contained to be true.

Sworn and subscribed before the 10th day of January 1850.

Adam Haun
Justice of the Peace of Blount County   John Henry
                                                 Samuel Henry

****

Personally appeared Ellenor Harris aged sixty four years, in August last of the County of Blount in the State of Tennessee, before the Court of said County, being a court of record, and being duly sworn according to law, on her oath says, that she has been acquainted with Mary Keeble whose name is subscribed to for the foregoing declaration ever since she and affiant were young girls, and before her marriage, that she the said Mary Keeble, married in Fauquier County in the State of Virginia, in the month of December 1799 and before Christmas of that month to William Keeble, who was represented to have been a soldier with affiants father Andrew Smith and to have served together with him the War of the Revolution.

Affiant was present at the marriage and saw and heard the said Mary married to the said William Keeble by John Pickett, a minister of the Gospel of the Baptist Order at the time above stated and before the second day of January 1800. Viz: in the month of December preceding, as afore stated by affiant. Affiant has heard read the foregoing declaration of the said Mary Keeble and believes the statements therein contained to be true, most of which stated by her as of her own knowledge, affiant knows to be true.

Sworn to and subscribed in open court this fifth day of November 1849.

                                                 Her
Robert A. Tedford, Clerk   Ellenor (X) Harris
                                                 Mark

State of Tennessee
Blount County

On this 29th day of March One Thousand Eight Hundred and Fifty Five
personally appeared before me John Clarke, an acting Justice of the Peace
for the county and State aforesaid Mary Keeble aged about seventy one
years a resident of Blount County in the State of Tennessee, who being
duly sworn according to law, declares that she is the widow of William
Keeble deceased who was a private in the Company commanded by
Captain Elias Edmonds in the Regiment of Virginia Troops commanded by
_____ in the Revolutionary War, that her said husband
enlisted under Edmonds and she believes was actively engaged as a
Soldier in said war for and during several Tours of Service, in fact she says
that her said husband spoke of serving for several years, he enlisted in
Fauquier County Virginia, she further state that her said husband, William
in the year 1832 and continued to draw a pension until he died, that she
was put on the pension list at ninety six dollars per annum on the eight of
February 1850, her pension commenced on the 4th of March 1848 under
the Act of Congress passed July 29th 1848 and that she is now the receipt
of said annuity. She further declares that she was married to the said
William Keeble in Fauquier County, Virginia on the seventeenth day of
December 1799 by John Picket a Minister of the Gospel that her name
before her said marriage was Mary Keeble, that she does not know of any
public or private record of the same, that her said husband died in Blount
county on the _____ day of December 1834, that she is now a widow.

She further declares that her said husband William Keeble never received
any Bounty Land whatever, either from the government of the United
States or from any other source within her knowledge. She therefore
makes this declaration for the purpose of obtaining the Bounty Land to
which she may be entitled under the Act of Congress approved March 3,
1855.

Her
Mary (X) Keeble
Mark

We James Henry and Soloman Farmer residents of the County of Blount
and State of Tennessee upon our oaths declare that the foregoing
Declaration was signed and acknowledged by Mary Keeble in our presence

and that we believe from the appearance and statements of the applicant that she is the identical person she represents herself to be.

We further swear that we have known said Mary Keeble for a great many years that we knew her in the life time of her said husband, William Keeble, and for years before his death she and her said husband lived and co-habitated together as husband and wife and were reputed as such, that they raised a considerable family of children all of whom are now grown and some of them residing near her, one of whom now living with her is probably fifty years of age and has always been understood and believed to be the son of the said William and Mary Keeble, we further swear that said Mary Keeble is now entitled to that which she seeks.

(You will note on page 66 that Mary was finally assigned a Bounty Land Warrant in January 1858 but alas, she had died in 1855 and the Warrant was not given to the heirs.)

An interesting fact here is that William had been given Bounty Land by the State of Virginia for his service. The land was in present day West Virginia in Greenbriar County. This Warrant was issued in 1784 the same year Mary was born, thus she had no knowledge of the grant. William sold his rights and probably never mentioned the transaction again.

WILL OF MARY KEEBLE

Will Book 1 Page 86
Blount County, Tennessee

In the name of God, Amen:

I, Mary Keeble of the County of Blount and State of Tennessee being in the seventy first year of my natural life with my proper mind to dispose of my goods and chattels do make this my last will and testament.

In the first place I will and bequeath my soul to the God of Mercies and my body to be interred in the tomb in a Christian manner.

In the second place my will is that all my just debts shall be paid out of my estate.

In the third place I will and bequeath to my daughter Jane have my mare named Rache and my large red bedstead with all the furniture pertaining to the bed and five calico quilts and one white counterpin, also the small chest.

In the fourth place I will and bequeath to my daughter Rebecca Farmer have my plain calico quilt.

In the fifth place I will and bequeath to my granddaughter Mary <u>Kerr</u>? Dunlap one counterpin.

In the sixth place I will and bequeath that all my property that remains shall be sold and equally divided amongst my children.

I appoint Soloman Farmer executor of my estate.
The 15th of June 1855

Her
Mary (X) Keeble
Mark

Test: William Henry
Vance Walker

64

SETTLEMENT OF THE ESTATE OF MARY KEEBLE-SOURCE-WILL BIN – BLOUNT COUNTY COURTHOUSE

To William (McCutchin) Keeble for year 1855 Mary Keeble, Dec'd.

June 20, 1857   Payment of $4.00   8 days work at .50¢ a day
****

August 31, 1858 P. S. Receipts have been filed from Walter Keeble, Jane H. Keeble and for bequests made to them.

Subpoena for W. Keeble Heirs. Issued Nov. 1857. Executed by notifying Soloman Farmer & wife, Stephen Davis & wife, Jane Keeble and Samuel Keeble
Nov. 18, 1857   C. Gillespy, Sheriff
****

Dec. 1, 1857: Thomas Keeble says with the Will amend of William Keeble, Dec'd. making oath that in executing said Will it became necessary to take a trip to Virginia to look after some bequests specified in said Will. That on the seventeenth of June Last, he started to Virginia and was gone until September 11th. That in making said trip he spent the sum of seventy seven dollars and thirty seven cents. That the said sum was spent whilst acting in my official capacity was I believed for the interest there fit of the said estate, as said Will referred to certain legacy which were due from testators father and mother, and I not knowing the conditions or situation of said legacy, I deemed it my duty to go and look after it, and in my making said trip the amount aforesaid was expended. Signed. Thomas Keeble

Sworn and Subscribed 1st Day of December 1857. J. C. McCoy, Clerk.
****

Thomas Keeble from William's Estate
From an affidavit on file it will be seen that as Administrator has expended in making a trip to Virginia to look after the interests of the above Estate the sum of $77.37.

I have allowed him in this settlement $30.09 which is all that was in his hands of the Estate.

The settlement has been postponed from time to time from Dec. 1857 to this date. The heirs and legatees were duly satisfied.

Respectfully, J. C. McCoy, Clerk.
****

Soloman Farmer, Executor of Mary Keeble, Dec'd. makes oath that in executing the trust imposed upon him by the said Will he deemed it his duty to take a trip to Paducah, Ky. To look after a legacy which was, he was informed and believed was coming from the estate of Charles Keeble, Dec'd. that he started March 1st 1857 and came back March 12, 1857 and spent the sum of $40.00. That the trip was taken in good faith believing that it would be in the interest of said estate and that the amount aforesaid was the amount he was temporarily compelled to expend.   Soloman Farmer
Sworn to: December 2, 1857   W. A. Walker, DC.
****

February 27, 1858 Assets of said Estate inadequate to pay debts.
****

Aug. 31st. 1858
I have received the property devised to me in the last Will and Testament of William Keeble, Dec'd. 75 Acres of land, a colt and a yoke of Oxen. We have each received a bed and furniture also the proceeds of the house specified in William Keeble Last Will and Test. This Aug. 31st. 1858
                              Jane (X) Keeble

Polly B. (X) Davis
Samuel W. Henry attested.
****

April 22, 1868
Received of Soloman Farmer, Executor of Mary Keeble, Dec'd. sixteen dollars the amount in full of a Legacy coming from R. Enders, Administrator of Charles Keeble, Dec'd. this April 22, AD 1868.
                              Mary Murrin
Attest: Andrew B. McTeer   Int. Revenue
                              Inl'd.Exchange   5¢ stamp.
****

Note that at the late date of 1868 ten years after the settlement of the major part of the estate, Mary Murrin, daughter of Charlotte Keeble Murrin received some of her mother's portion of the grandmother's Estate. By this time she was of legal age to sign for herself.

#43.

State of Tennessee}   I., J. C. McCoy, Clerk of the County of said County
Blount County   }   have proceeded, after giving the notice required by
law to make settlement with Soloman Farmer, Exc.
Of Mary Keeble, Dec'd.

I find on examining the Records that said Farmer was qualified at August Term 1855 and I charge him as follows, Viz:
To amt. Of list of Sales Returned to Court in Nov. Term 1855 and due 29 June 1856

	$99.65
Int. collected on same	2.00
To Amt. Of list of Sales Returned to Court	
Jan. Term 1856 Due 7 June 1856	81.47
Int. Due on same	7.36
Amt Chargeable	————
	$190.48

Which Amt is subject to the following:
Disbursements-Viz:

No. 1.	Harmin and Henry	Recpt.	9.55
No. 2	J.N. Toole & Co.	Note	29.50
No. 3	William Keeble	Recpt.	4.00
No. 4	Andrew Peery	"	4.50
No. 5	Spencer Henry	"	.87
No. 6	Samuel Walker	"	4.50
No. 7	J. Stones	"	20.25
No. 8	Vance Walker	"	4.00
No. 9	A. L. Taylor	"	11.50
No. 10	J. C. Fagg & Sons	"	3.83
No. 11	J. M. Toole	"	50.53
No. 12	Exc.-Extra Services Tc.		52.00

Pg. 48:

No. 13	Exr's Account	4.00
No. 14	East Tennessee Money	2.00
	Extra Services	15.00
	Clerk Fees	7.30
	Clerk for Transcripts	2.50
	C. Gillespy's fees	1.25
	W. McTeer's fees	.50
	D. Taylor's fees	.25

$227.65

Being this amount $57.17

COURT SETTLEMENT WITH SOLOMAN FARMER
re: <u>MARY KEEBLE. Dec'd.</u>

December Term 1857
(Continued from Pg. 1 of Page 48 in Estate Book "D")

Overpaid by Executor said Extr. Has filed Receipts from Jane Keeble, Rebecca Farmer and Mary Ann Dunlap (See Vouchers 15-16-17) for certain articles of personal property and devised to them.

The Will thus having been complied with the debts and the assets are exhausted.

I consider this a FULL and FINAL SETTLEMENT of said Estate.
Respectfully Submitted,
J. C. McCoy Clk. By W. A. Walker, D.C.
December 1857.

Millen Francis
Treasurer of East Tennessee

Maryville, Tennessee
March 29, 1858
Commissioner of Pensions,

Sir:
Enclosed please find two Bounty Land Warrants, to wit: 160 Acre Warrant
No. 14518 issued 18th January 1858 to Mary Keeble, Widow of William
Keeble Private, Revolutionary War, and 80 Acre Warrant No. 37004 issued
24th June 1856 to Lucy Harris, Widow of James Harris, Private Captain
Tipton's Company, Tennessee, Militia War of 1812. These Warrants were
sent to me from the Department and I have learned that the claimants both
died before the issuance of the Warrants, and have therefore thought it my
duty to return them lest they might by some means get out of my
possession and give trouble to the Department if not to me.

Will you please acknowledge receipt of same so that I may satisfy the
children and heirs of the disposition I have made of them. There are no
minor children in either case.

Respectfully,
John E. Toole

DISPOSITION OF WILLIAM KEEBLE LANDS

Blount county Deeds Book JKL or #5 Pg. 392-3

December 26, 1834, <u>William Keeble & Walter H. Keeble</u> – Son of said William Keeble as well as for the natural love and affection which he hath and bear unto the said Walter H. Keeble, also for the better maintenance and preferment of the said Walter H. Keeble, his heirs and assigns all that tenement and piece, parcel or tract of land on waters of Little Ellejoy containing 75 Acres. To include 11-1/4 Acres of the new survey to run with Patton Alegis line to the mountain. Walter is to have 63 ¾ Acres of the east end of the 250 Acre tract that the above William Keeble now lives on running equal distance to NE corner south 63 ¾ Acres and no more; and He the said Walter H. Keeble is to stay on the farm and cultivate it in the best way that he can for to make support for the family for two years, and at the end of two years he is to have possession of the 25 Acres of land above named and not before – together with all the appurtenances and belongings.

	His
Vance Walker	William (X) Keeble
Rachel Henry	Mark
William McTeer	Witnesses sworn to the above
	March 24, 1835
	Registered April 21, 1835

Blount County Deeds Book Y Pg. 257

February 17, 1840 <u>Walter H. Keeble to Thomas Keeble</u> – I Walter H. Keeble bargained and sold and transfer, convey to Thomas Keeble for one hundred and fifteen dollars 14th District estimated 75 acres and 11 ¼ acres of the new survey to run with Potter Elages line to the mountain, the 45 Acres to be divided into 4 equal parts and Walter H. to have the fourth next to Patton Elegas line to and including the spring that is in a few chains of the Lick Branch, and the said Walter H. is to have 63 ¾ Acres of the East End of the 25 Acre tract that the above William Keeble now lives on, running on equal distance from the NE and SE Corner so that a straight line across the old survey will make the 63 ¾ Acres and no more, and if the line should take in the spring that is on the Dry Branch below the bluff that I reserve with the lands that lie adjoining south of the spring – the Old Field – land described in Deed of Gift from William Keeble to Walter H. Keeble.

Witnesses: Sam Henry, Sr.	Walter H. Keeble
Sam Henry, Jr.	Received Aug. 6, 1855

DEED BPPL 'Y' BLOUNT COUNTY TENNESSEE PAGE 310
(Sale of the Keeble Property after Death of Mary Keeble)

We, Soloman Farmer and wife Rebecca Farmer, formerly Rebecca Keeble, one of the heirs at law of William Keeble, deceased, and Jane H. Keeble, also one of the heirs at law of said William Keeble and Joseph Anderson Dunlap, who also is representing Hannah Dunlap and her husband Joseph Dunlap, said Hannah being formerly Hannah Keeble, also one of the heirs of William Keeble, deceased, have this day sold and do hereby transfer, convey and forever quit claim to Walter H. Keeble and his heirs forever for $24.50 to us the said Soloman and Rebecca Farmer and $24.50 to me the said Jane H. and $50.00 to me said Joseph A. Dunlap, all our several interests and undisputed shares in the land which descended to us from William Keeble, deceased, being each of us 1/10th part of said land joining the lands of Sam Henry, Samuel Walker, Thomas Keeble, Asah Henry with one John Henry and others containing 220 Acres be of same, more or less, and said land is the land upon which Mrs. Mary Keeble lately died said land having been willed to her, said Mary Keeble, widow of said William Keeble during her lifetime and at her death to his heirs specified in his will.

August 13, 1855

Soloman Farmer
Rebecca Farmer
Jane H. Keeble
Joseph A. Dunlap

You will note that the Estate was divided into ten shares. There are only nine signatures to the following sale of the land.

Charlotte Keeble Murrin had died in 1847. Her only heir, Mary Murrin, was not yet of age to accept her mother's share of the estate.

It would appear that Andrew J. Murrin, who was appointed her guardian, would have signed the transaction in her behalf, but that was not the case.

Mary Murrin's share of the Estate probably had to be filed thru the Chancery Court after her father was approved as her Guardian, she being a Minor. We were unable to find that Chancery Court Record.

Blount County Deeds Book Y Pg. 297
December 10, 1855 3-1/2 O'Clock P.M. Manley Keeble to Samuel Yearout

I, Manley Keeble have this day bargained and sold and hereby transfer and convey to Samuel Yearout and his heirs and assigns forever my entire interest which is 1/10th in a certain tract or parcel of land, situated lying and being in Blount County, State of Tennessee 14th District on the waters of Ellejoy Creek and adjoining the lands with the heirs of John Henry, Samuel Henry, Samuel Walker, Thomas Keeble, the heirs of John Henry to the beginning containing 186 Acres more or less. The above described land being that of which William Keeble lived and died.

Manley Keeble

(I am justly indebted to Clemmentine Saffell, guardian of the heirs of John Saffell, Dec'd. in the sum of $60.00 and Mose Gamble is my security for payment of same . . .)

Blount County Deeds Book Z Pg. 575
February 17, 1860 <u>Keeble Heirs to Samuel W. Henry and Josias Gamble</u>
We, Thomas Keeble, Samuel Keeble, Manley Keeble and Richard Keeble for ourselves and Walter H. Keeble, for myself, and Hannah Dunlap, formerly Hannah Keeble and Soloman Farmer and Rebecca Farmer, his wife, formerly Rebecca Keeble and Stephen Davis and Mary Davis, his wife, formerly Mary Keeble and Jane Keeble, heirs of William Keeble, Dec'd. have this day bargained and sold and do hereby convey to Samuel W. Henry and Josias Gamble of the County of Blount and State of Tennessee for the sum of one thousand and one hundred dollars to us in hand paid, the receipt of which is hereby acknowledged a certain piece, parcel or tract of land lying and being situated in the County of Blount and State of Tennessee in the 14th Civil District of said county on the waters of Ellejoy Creek and adjoining the lands of Samuel Henry, the heirs of Samuel Walker, Dec'd., Thomas Keeble and others, containing one hundred and eighty seven and one fourth Acres – also another tract or parcel of land adjoining said tract just described, Samuel W. Henry. Thomas Keeble and others containing thirty three and three-fourths Acres being part of lands formerly owned by William Keeble, Dec'd. and being the same lands said William Keeble died seized and possessed of. We do covenant with the said Samuel W. Henry and Josias Gamble that we are lawfully seized and possessed of said land as the heirs of said William Keeble, Dec'd. and that we have a good right to convey the same and that it is un-incumbered. We do further covenant and bind ourselves, our heirs and representatives to warrant and defend the right to said land and every part there of to the said Samuel Henry and Josias Gamble and their heirs and representatives

forever against the lawful claims of all persons what so ever. In Witness there of we have hereto set our hands and seals on this seventeenth day of February in the year of our Lord One Thousand Eight Hundred and Sixty.

Signed in presence of us   Thomas Keeble
Day and Date above written   Samuel Keeble
John Gamble   Manual (X) Keeble
H. J. Henry   Richard (X) Keeble
                                 Walter (X) Keeble

With the completion of the above sale, the lands of William Keeble, Dec'd. were completely disbursed from the Estate.

No thought had been given about the retention of that part of the Estate which had become a family cemetery.

First buried there was Charlotte Keeble White, sister of Mary Keeble. Her death was prior to her father's death in 1811. (Her marker has no dates)

We know from earlier information that Charlotte and Wilson White had a home in the vicinity of William and Mary's home, because of Wilson White's Land Grant. However, tradition tells us that Charlotte was being cared for in her last illness by her sister Mary. Charlotte looked up the hill from the Keeble home and requested that she be buried up on the hillside, visible from the cabin, by a large fir tree. It was thought that she was dying of tuberculosis.

William Keeble, infant son of Manly and Rebecca Keeble, was there, after being born and died on October 25, 1832.

William Keeble himself was buried there in 1834.

Charlotte Keeble Murrin, wife of A. J. Murrin, was interred in 1847. Mary Keeble was interred in 1855.

We do not know the death date of Sally Keeble Boling and she probably was buried there prior to 1867 when members of the family realized that they had sold the final resting place of their loved ones.

With this sudden realization that they had no control over the cemetery, A. J. Murrin, John S. Boling, and Soloman Farmer initiated legal proceedings to return this part of the original Keeble lands to the family.

They purchased the land from Samuel W. Henry, original purchaser of the Keeble Estate for $5.00. They started legal proceedings on October 25, 1867, after the Civil War.

Final Registry at the Blount County Courthouse was completed November 11, 1867.

Many of the Keebles listed in this book and their extended families are resting here in the Keeble Graveyard.

Deed of Conveyance-Samuel W. Henry to A. J. Murrin & Richard Keeble

This Indenture made and entered into on the twenty fifth day of October 1867 Between Samuel W. Henry of the County of Blount and State of Tennessee of the one part and A. J. Murrin & Richard Keeble Trustees of the County and State aforesaid of the other part Witnesseth that the said Samuel W. Henry for and in consideration of the sum of five dollars to him in hand paid the Receipt of Which is hereby acknowledged hath granted, bargained and sold and by these presents doth Grant bargain and Sell unto the said A. J. Murrin and Richard Keeble, Trustees and to their successors for ever a certain piece, parcel or tract of land situated in the County of Blount on the Farm known as the Keeble Farm Containing One halfacre and bounded as follows To wit: Beginning at a Stake the South East etc...to the beginning. To have and hold the said piece parcel or Tract of Land with all and singular its appertances Benefits hereditiaments and privileges in any wise belonging or appertaining there into unto the said A. J. Murrin and Richard Keeble, Trustees and their Successors forever for the proper use of a publick grave yard and the said Samuel W. Henry by this indenture for himself and his heirs. Executors and administrators do warrant and defend the said Tract of land unto the said A. J. Murrin and Richard Keeble, Trustees and their Successors against the Claim and demand of all and every person or persons whatsoever. In witness Where of the said Samuel W. Henry hath hereto set his hand and affixt his seal the day and year above written.
Signed Sealed and Acknowledged in the presence of:

John S. Boling   S. W. Henry
Soloman Farmer

State of Tennessee
Blount County

Personally came John S. Boling and Soloman Farmer subscribing Witnesses to the foregoing deed ...who being duly sworn say they are well acquainted with S. W. Henry the bargainor and that they saw him execute the same for the purposes there in contained.
Given under my hand this Nov. 11, 1867

R. E. Tedford

State of Tennessee: I, R. E. Tedford, Register Clerk Blount County for said County rec'd the foregoing deed Nov. 11th 1 ½ PM 1867 as entered in Note Book B Page 55th and registered the same in Book 2nd. B Page 454 of my office.

Witness my hand at office this 11th day of Nov. 1867.

R. E. Tedford
Reg.

THOMAS KEEBLE
1800 – 1873

THE

HOLY BIBLE,

CONTAINING

THE OLD AND NEW TESTAMENTS:

TRANSLATED OUT OF

THE ORIGINAL TONGUES,

AND WITH THE

FORMER TRANSLATIONS DILIGENTLY COMPARED AND REVISED.

STEREOTYPE EDITION.

NEW-YORK:

STEREOTYPED BY A. CHANDLER,

FOR THE AMERICAN BIBLE SOCIETY.
....
1830.

Nonpareil 12mo.]

William Newton
was born in 1755 —
May 21st 1756 —

A

B

Thomas Keeble was Born
July the 31 st 1800

Elizabeth his wife

Elizabeth Keeble his wife
was born Aug the 1805

Thomas H. Keeble was born
Dec the 14 th 1824

H. B. Keeble was
born March the 10 th 1827

Keeble was born
January the 14 th 1829

Thomas J. Keeble was born
Feb the 16 th 1831

Keeble was born
Feb the 14 th 1833

Mary Keeble Born
Nov 15 1845

Robert Marion Keeble
was Born September
25 th 1850

John Anderson
Keeble was born
the 17 May 1853

Alfred Henry Keeble
was born November
1855

1865

Thomas Keeler —
Departed This life
August 25 - 1873.
Aged 73 years

O B B Bourt

1881

E

THOMAS KEEBLE

Thomas Keeble of Blount County, Tennessee, was born July 31, 1800, as recorded in his mother's Bible, the son of William Keeble and Mary (Keeble) Keeble. He was born seven months after the marriage of his parents. The family had just arrived in Blount County in the spring of 1800 from Fauquier County, Virginia, thus it was an arduous journey for his mother who was sixteen years of age and pregnant. The father was forty-six years of age.

Mary's Declaration to obtain a Widow's Pension quoted her as saying that they moved to Blount County, Tennessee, in the spring of 1800. She states that they settled in Blount County and remained there. (This would be the present day area near Walland, Tennessee.) Thus it would appear that Thomas was born near the site of the present day Keeble Chapel and graveyard.

According to Mr. Sam Humphreys, who lived near the church prior to his death several years ago, the William Keeble cabin was located down in a glen across the present road from the church and cemetery. At the site there was water from a stream and a coal vein, the latter being mentioned in the Deed.

We must assume that Thomas and his ten brothers and sisters were raised there. On October 14, 1823, Thomas married Elizabeth Smith, daughter of Joseph Smith and Margaret (McCutchin) Smith. Their marriage bond is on record at the Blount County Courthouse. Margaret's father, Joseph, was a Veteran of the War of 1812 – a Private in Capt. Samuel Thompson's Company, Col. Edwin Booth's Regiment in the East Tennessee Militia. He served from November 13, 1814, to May 18, 1815, when he was discharged. He was deceased by 1816 prior to Margaret's marriage. Joseph was the son of John Smith of Pennsylvania.

Margaret's parents were Samuel and Elizabeth (Fulton) McCutchin of Augusta County, Virginia. Their marriage is recorded in Augusta County as March 11, 1800. We have no idea as to whether Tom and Elizabeth continued to live on at the home with his parents, or hers, or whether they were permitted to build a cabin on the homeplace. There appears to be no apparent transfer of land to Thomas, or any of his brothers or sisters, until William wrote his Will four days prior to his death December 30, 1834. In the Will, written December 26th, according to the Deed "Willim Keeble and Walter H. Keeble, son of said William – for the natural love and affection which he hath and bear unto the said Walter H. Keeble" he gives 75 acres, including the homeplace. Walter is to stay on the land and cultivate it for two years. Deed Book #5 Pg. 392-393. Registered at the courthouse April 21, 1835. On February 17, 1840 in Deed Book "Y" Pg. 257, Walter H. Keeble sold to Thomas the same 75 acres describing in the Gift Deed originally given to Walter H. by his father.

Thus if Thomas had built a cabin on or near the original homeplace, he now owned it as of February 1840. This cabin is probably the one from which Mr. J. H. Farmer secured the Will of Mary Keeble's father when the Thomas Keeble cabin was torn down in the early 1900s. It certainly was not the original William Keeble homeplace, as it was not down in the glen. Ella Farmer showed us where the Thomas Keeble cabin sat – near her home – it was identifiable by the pile of chimney rocks still on the site.

It is interesting to note that the 175 acres remaining of the original 250 acres was not divided among the children until after their Mother's death in 1855. Thomas, of course, received a 1/10th interest in that remaining land.

In the 1829 Declaration to the government in order to obtain a pension, William states that heretofore he has been able to support himself by the assistance of his children, who have lately left him. He then lists the children still at home – Rebecca (age 19), Richard (now 18), Walter (age 13), Polly (Mary) (age 10), Charlotte (age 5), and Jane (about 4). Thus, those who have recently left home are Thomas, Samuel, Hannah, and Manly. William stated in the Declaration of 1829 that Walter is sickly, so Richard (age 18) is the only male left at home to assist his father.

We can surmise that Thomas, being the oldest, lived nearby to assist his father and mother as best he could. We know that Thomas had possession of a horse belonging to his father at the time William's Will was written, which would tend to confirm their cooperation in farming the land.

Thomas and Elizabeth had five children: James H. Keeble, born December 4, 1824, who married Mary A. Sneed, daughter of Taylor Sneed and Frances _____ in Blount County on February 25, 1844. William McCutchin Keeble, born March 1, 1827, who married 1st Mary Tounsel (Townsend?) in Blount County on November 20, 1845, and 2nd

Nancy Jenkins in Sevier County on August 14, 1862. Joseph H. Keeble, born January 4, 1829 (who is unknown to us), Thomas J. Keeble, born February 16, 1831 (who is also unknown to us) and Mary Keeble, born March 4, 1833, and who married John S. Boling on January 12, 1853, in Blount County, Tennessee.

Elizabeth (Smith) Keeble died prior to 1847, for in that year Thomas married Nancy Ann Cannon, daughter of John Cannon and Nancy _____. They were married on February 16, 1847, also in Blount County. The 1860 Census states that Nancy Ann was 39 years old, which would make her birthdate about 1821. Mother Cannon, age 78, was living with Thomas and Nancy Ann.

Mr. Joe Farmer, a Blount County native who later moved to Seattle, Washington, advised me that Nancy Ann Cannon had lived near Uncle Walter (Watt) Keeble with her mother, Polly, and a sister. He stated that they had a sheep farm. Mr. Farmer also stated that it was common knowledge that Nancy Ann had a bad temper.

Docie Keeble related that his grandmother (Nancy Ann) and her family lived in the Liberty Area of Blount County. This would be relatively near Uncle Watt, who lived in the Cloyd's Creek-Friendsville area of Blount County.

Docie remembered visiting his grandmother, Nancy Ann Keeble, at the Thomas Keeble cabin near William Keeble's home. He described it as a typical log cabin externally, with pine walls within. The chimney on one end of the cabin was built "head high" out of stone and clay and above that with sticks and clay. The puncheon floor was made of poplar boards varying in widths – actually the width of the tree the boards were cut from. These boards were four to five inches thick. Under the cabin was a "root" cellar for storage of potatoes and other vegetables. The access to the cellar was through a trap door in the floor, which raised up to permit entry. He did not remember an external entry to the cellar.

Thomas's cabin was located on a rise in the land just to the left of the cabin where Sis and Elly Farmer's cabin stood. I would assume that their cabin was Eli Farmer's cabin before the children inherited it. I do not know if the latter cabin is still standing. It was there 15 or 20 years ago. The only evidence of the site of Tom's cabin is an ivy-covered pile of rocks which once comprised the chimney and foundation stones.

Docie's grandmother lived in the Thomas Keeble cabin until about 1896, when Docie was four or five years of age. She apparently then lived with Alford or "Pid," as Docie's father was called. Grandmother Nancy Ann died and was buried at Liberty Baptist Cemetery. She had an old maid sister, Aunt Cindy, who moved in with Pid to care for the children, but this didn't work out and Cindy was taken to the Poor Farm, where she died about 1897.

Children of the second marriage of Thomas were: Eliza Jane Keeble, born February 15, 1848, who married Eli Farmer on August 13, 1868, in Blount County. Robert Marion Keeble, born September 25, 1850, and who died in his teens with "brain fever." John Anderson Keeble, born July 17, 1853, and who married Sarah Davis on December 25, 1882, in Blount County. Alford Henry Keeble, born November 7, 1855, and who married first Millie Jane Davis about 1876. His second wife was Rachel F. Donaldson, who he married on January 19, 1886, in Blount County, Tennessee. At the time of the 1860 Census, Eliza Jane was 12 years old. Robert M. was 10, John Anderson 6, and "Pid" was 5.

Docie related that his "Grandpa Tommy" was a horse doctor. Tommy's theory concerning the use of medicine for farm animals was, "A little do good, alot do better." Aunt Polly Helton, granddaughter of Thomas, knew him also and said he was a "natural" around animals. He was a good veterinarian for his day and was sought after for treating animals. She stated there were no doctors in the community close at hand, and Tommy's expertise with animals carried over into human illnesses so that people came to him with their medical problems in their desperation for advice and relief.

One of the prescriptions, which Polly told me was for earache and which one of my children had at the time of my visit, was the following: Go out into the woods and grub around some oak trees until you find a black beetle – separate the head from the body of the beetle and squeeze the body part into the ear. I've often wondered if there is some medicinal quality there that science should be made aware of, but rest assured I did not get a black beetle to treat my daughter's earache.

W. H. Keeble, Professor of Physics at Randolph-Macon College in Ashland, Virginia, wrote me in 1954: "About my Uncle Tom – My father tells enough stories about him to fill a book. He must have been a very eccentric character."

Both Docie and "Si" Keeble (the latter being W. H.'s brother) stated that Tommy was deaf in his old age. Since he didn't hear questions asked of him, Nancy Ann, "The Mrs.," would answer all questions directed to Tom. He was known to swear "Once in awhile."

One of the surviving tales about Thomas and related to me by "Si" Keeble is as follows:

Tommy was working in his cornfield and Jim Summey's dog was in the field with him. The dog was making a nuisance of himself, lying on the young corn plants and scratching in the dirt. Tommy wanted rid of the dog but the animal would not pay any attention to the commands to leave the field.

There was a group of fox hunters, with dogs, who had chased a fox all night and well into the day. Tom tried to get the dog to join the hunt, to follow the dogs. One hunter came by and Tom yelled to him "That's the biggest fox I ever saw"! A second hunter passed and Tom yelled to him, "They've run through my field four times already." Each time Tom tried to entice the dog to join the excitement. When the next hunter appeared, Tom hollered in exasperation, "If Jim Summey's dog were my dog, I'd kill him, damn him."

When Thomas's father died in 1834, he named his wife as his Executrix of his estate. When wife Mary died, she named her son-in-law, Soloman Farmer, a Justice of the Peace, as her Executor. Mary died in 1855 and in that same year Thomas decided that he should make a trip to Fauquier County, Virginia, to determine what the inheritance might be that his father had mentioned in his Will that the children could expect from both sides of their grandparents' lines. One would think that it would have been Soloman's duty to go, but apparently Thomas went with the blessings of his brothers and sisters, as well as the Court.

In his report to the Court upon his return, Thomas advised that he left home on the 17th of June and was gone until September 11. In making the trip, he expended the sum of $70.30. There was only $30.37 in the hands of the Executrix at the time of her death on June 15. The sum at hand was authorized to be given to Thomas by J. C. McCoy, Clerk of the Court, on December 1, 1857.

Thomas reported to the Court that he was unable to find any inheritance due from his grandparents' estates. This statement would confirm how completely the older generation had kept the children from knowing of William's past. It would appear to me that Thomas went only to Virginia and probably should have gone to Maryland to seek the inheritance (this is mere conjecture on my part).

Aunt Polly Helton stated that years later, about 1912, as best she could recollect, someone came through on horseback looking for the heirs of William and Mary Keeble, but the members of the family who were approached knew nothing of their ancestors and didn't make an effort to locate anyone in the family who had that knowledge. The younger generation did not even ascertain where the person seeking Keeble kinfolk had come from. The entire episode left only frustration for Aunt Polly.

According to Aunt Polly, who calculated time by the use of things like, "The bad winter of 1867" or "the year of the big flood." Thomas died on August 25, 1875, when Polly was about eleven years of age. Estate Book "F" in the Blount County Clerks Office, Page 21, has a notation to the Court held on the first Monday of September 1874 that "Thomas Keeble died intestate."

Aunt Polly states that Thomas was buried in Keeble Chapel Cemetery, which was near his home. She assumed that Elizabeth Smith Keeble, the first wife, was buried there also, as Elizabeth died at home, as best Polly knew. There are no grave markers for either grave. Polly's comment was, "You know, in those days they didn't haul bodies all over the county like they do now." One must assume that both Elizabeth and Thomas were buried in Keeble Cemetery because it was "near home."

Among the several Deeds regarding the settlement of Thomas's Estate is one from Deed Book #47, Page 18. "This Indenture made this 15th of November 1894 between John S. Boling and his wife of Sevier County and John A. Keeble and Alford H. Keeble of Blount County second part . . . $90.00 old Thomas Keeble tract. Said tract descended to the heirs of

Thomas Keeble, one part to Mary (Boling) by inheritance one part to Mary by purchase from brother William."

STATE OF TENNESSEE #29596

TO ALL TO WHOM THESE PRESENTS SHALL COME:

KNOW YE. That in consideration of an ENTRY made in the ENTRY TAKER's OFFICE of Blount County of No. 1502 dated 2nd day of April 1855 by Thomas Keeble there is GRANTED by the State of Tennessee unto the said Thomas Keeble and his heirs a certain TRACT of LAND containing thirty-three acres lying in the County aforesaid on the WATERS OF Little River beginning at a stake corner to the occupant survey of William Keeble thence with the same North forty-one East nine chains to a stake. South seventy five East fifteen and eight North Chains to a Poplar Stump corner to William Keeble's Entry thence with the same South thirty-nine West eleven and five tenths links to a stake, South forty nine..East twenty-four and five tenths Chains to a stake. North forty East thirty and five tenths Chains to a double chestnut. Corner of James Walker thence with the same North forty-five and a half East sixty Chains to a stake corner Vance Walker thence with the same North forty-five and a half East sixty Chains to a stake corner James Walker thence with the same North forty-five and a half East sixty Chains to a stake corner Vance Walker thence with the same North fifty-seven East one and one tenths Chains to a Stake. South forty-two East two and eight tenths Chains to a stake in a line of J. H. Gillespies thence with the same, North forty West one hundred and three Chains to a stake corner of J. H. Gillespies one hundred thirty-two and a half. Thence with the same North forty nine West twenty-four and three-tenths Chains to a stake. South fifty-five West sixteen Chains to a stake on a line of Samuel Walkers line with the same North thirty-five West eighteen and seven tenths Chains to a small black oak North thirty-five West fifteen and five tenths Chains to the Beginning.

Surveyed February 25th, 1856

With its appurtenances, to HAVE and to HOLD the same TRACT or PARCEL of LAND with its appurtenances to the said Thomas Keeble and his heirs forever. IN WITNESS WHEREOF, Andrew Johnson Governor of the State of Tennessee, has hereunto set his hand and caused the Great Seal of the State to be affixed at NASHVILLE on the 23rd day of May in the

YEAR OF OUR LORD one thousand eight hundred and fifty six and of
AMERICAN INDEPENDENCE 80th.

Andrew Johnson

F.N.W. Burton, SECRETARY

On reverse side: Certified copy
County: Blount
No. 29596
Book: East 30
Page: 324
Type record: Land Grant Tenn. State Library and
Archives

To John Gamble, Greetings:

Where as it has been reported to us in our County Court opened and held for the County of Blount, State of Tennessee at the Court House in Maryville on the 1st Monday of September 1874 that THOMAS KEEBLE, late of said County had died intestate having whilst living and at the time of his death Goods & Chattels & Rights and Credits the ordering and granting Administration where of doth appertain unto us and we being desirous that said Goods & Chattels Rights & Credits may be well administered do grant unto you the said John Gamble full power by these presents to collect and take unto your possession all and singular the Goods & Chattels Rights & Credit which were of the said Thomas Keeble, Dec'd. at the time of his death where so ever the name may be found hereby requiring you to make, or cause to be made and returned to our said Court at its next term a true and perfect inventory of said Goods & Chattels, Rights & Credits and also to render a clear and true account of said administration where there of required.

Witness: J. A. Greer, Clerk of said Court at Offices in Maryville on the first Monday of September 1874.

J. A. Greer, Clerk

Your author is indebted to Mrs. Patricia Keeble Noble, Dec'd, formerly of San Antonio, Texas, for the descendants of James H. and Mary Sneed Keeble. We knew that Thomas had a son, James H. Keeble, from the Thomas Keeble Bible record, but we had no knowledge of his line prior to receiving correspondence from Mrs. Noble. Her first letter to me was inquiring if I had any knowledge of the ancestor of James H. Keeble and was there a possibility of any connection with her "line?" We were thrilled to be able to give her two generations back and found an entire line to add to our Keeble genealogy. "Pat" made an early sketch of her ancestors and forwarded it to me saying that she would "fill in the blanks" as she found additional family members. She had made two trips back to East Tennessee to meet kinfolk and view the area from which her ancestors had migrated.

Mrs. Noble sent me a history of her family from the time they left Blount County until the time when she awakened to "family" other than in Texas. I quote, "John Houston Keeble's father, James H. Keeble, married Mary A.

Sneed on February 25th, 1844. They had ten children. John Houston was the eldest in the 1860 Census. The family was living in Catoosa County, Georgia. On February 16, 1863, John Houston enlisted in Company 1 of 1st Confederate Regiment of Georgia Volunteers. He was wounded in the right foot at the battle of Franklin in Tennessee on November 30, 1864. He was captured on December 17th 1864, when Federal Troops overran the Confederate rear guard and captured the wounded as southern troops retreated from their defeat at Nashville. John Houston was forwarded to Louisville, Kentucky, where he remained as a prisoner until his release on June 17th, 1865, after he pledged his allegiance to the U.S. Government.

His family, whose farm was located on what became a part of the battleground near Chattanooga, lost all their belongings when a fire swept the battlefield killing Confederate and Yankee troops alike. John Houston was released to Rock Mills in Randolph County Alabama where the family had relocated in his absence. There he married Martha Caroline Muldrew and fathered four children: James Taylor, John David, William LaFayette and Mary Caroline. The mother, Martha Caroline died in 1875 in Alabama and John Houston subsequently married Martha Carolines' widowed sister Amarinthia Susan Muldrew Cook. They moved to Henderson County Texas about 1878 where they lived on a Caney Creek farm. John Houston died in 1882 and is buried in an unmarked grave at Old Sand Flat Cemetery. Amarintha Susan provided for all five children by operating an apple mill in Henderson County, Texas."

F.II. SAMUEL KEEBLE
B: 3/2/1802
D: 9/ /1869

SAMUEL KEEBLE
March 2, 1802 – September 1869

Samuel Keeble, the second son of William Keeble, Revolutionary War Veteran and his wife, Mary Keeble, was born March 2, 1802, according to the record in his mother's Bible. As I have related in his older brother, Thomas's biography, Samuel was raised with the other Keeble children in a log cabin down in a glen near the Keeble Chapel in the Walland Community of Blount County, Tennessee.

We know nothing of the physical features of the man other than the tradition related in Manly's biography that Samuel, with his brothers Thomas, Manly, and Richard, would have weighed over one thousand pounds, combined weight. Our subject would have left home prior to 1829, when his father made a declaration to the government in order to obtain a pension. His father did not list him among the children still living at home.

Mr. Keeble did not marry. He was a farmer in the community in which he lived. As with so many individuals who do not marry, or if married, do not leave heirs, information about them is sketchy. If one is prominent in politics or war, such as George Washington, heirs are not necessary for notoriety. Usually ministers or school teachers who have made an impact on a community are remembered for their intellect or their services to mankind. Here we have a subject, a single man, a farmer without cause for notoriety, in fact, Mr. "Si" (Edgar) Keeble states that Samuel was not as astute mentally as the other members of the family, according to what he had always heard related about Samuel in the family.

William H. Keeble, Professor of Physics at Randolph Macon College in Ashland, Virginia, an older brother of "Si" said it very well when he stated in a letter to me on March 29, 1958, "None of us (Keebles) with the exception of John Bell Keeble of Nashville ever became noted or notorious and the trails of most of those who have gone before are rather dim." About Samuel in particular he said, "Uncle Sam never married. My father told many anecdotes in connection with Uncle Sam. He must have been as eccentric as Uncle Tom."

Sam inherited 25 acres of his father's property and apparently already had outstanding debts which left him landless.

Deed Book Y, Page 562, in the Blount County Clerks Office in Maryville, I, Samuel Keeble, Blount County, State of Tennessee sold to A. M. Henry for one dollar and other considerations, a Tract on Little Ellejoy Creek in the 14th Civil District my undivided interest in the old William Keeble Tract of land joining the lands of Sam'l Henry, Sr., Sam'l Walker, Sr., and others containing twenty five (25) acres more or less, but this deed made to A. M. Henry as trustee to secure to Hammond and Henry the sum of $67.75 due to them by note of hand dated 26th Feb. 1857, bearing interest from date which debt I wish to secure and make certain unto said Hammonds and Henry. If I shall pay the debt and every part thereof in 12 months from date, then this is to be void. If I fail, Trustee to advertise said land at five (5) public places in said County and proceed to sell said land for ready money to the highest bidder, and pay said debt and expenses and costs and balance to me if there be any."

Samuel Keeble

Witnessed: Soloman Farmer
            William Farmer   Feb. 27, 1857

It would appear that Samuel moved to Sevier County, Tennessee shortly after this sale and rented a farm in the 10th District of Sevier County for the remainder of his life.

In my October 1952 interview with Mary Martin (Polly) Keeble Helton, who was ninety one years old at the time, she advised that her Father, Mother, and she moved to Sevier County from Blount County in 1865 when she was two years old. Apparently Samuel was already a resident of Sevier County at that time. According to Polly, Samuel lived alone and "batched" it, meaning that he lived alone as a bachelor.

Polly stated that she was six years old when Samuel died. Her father, William McCutcheon Keeble, who was called "Cutch," brought Samuel to their home in his last illness, as he had no one to care for him.

Polly's mother was seven months pregnant with Polly's sister to be – Adaline. It was Polly's duty to take her little cedar bucket that had been made for her and get cool water from the spring that flowed near the house. She quenched Samuel's thirst and held a cool cloth to his fevered brow. It was also her chore to stand over him and wave a cloth or paper back and forth over his body to keep the flies away, as they had no screens in those days. Her other chore was to feed Samuel when he became too weak to care for himself. These duties of caring for a dying person at such an early age made an indelible impression on her memory. She related that his death occurred in September of 1869. His body, in its casket of wood, was taken in a farm wagon pulled by a horse to Shiloh Cemetery, Sevier County, where it was interred. The plot was marked with a cedar post, but no marker was ever raised.

SETTLEMENT OF THE ESTATE OF SAMUEL KEEBLE
Blount County Estate Book F, Pg. 4

A list of the property sold February 14, 1874, belonging to the estate of
SAMUEL KEEBLE, Sr. Dec'd, Sold on 6 months time

Purchaser	Property	Amount
W. C. Davis	1 Axe	.75
James Davis	10-1/2 # Frow # .06	.63
John Dunlap	2 Augers	.10
William Keeble	1 Gimlet	.10
William Keeble	1 Hoe	.35
James Farmer	2 Hammers	.45
James Davis	1 Chizel	.20
Thomas F. More	1 Feather Bed & Straw Tick	4.35
William Keeble	1 Handkerchief	.15
William Keeble	1 Shirt Front	.50
William Keeble	1 Pr. Slips	.37-1/2
William Keeble	2 Pr. Pants	.25
William Keeble	1 Coat	.50
William Keeble	2 Vests	.10
William Keeble	1 Summer Coat & Vest	.50
William Keeble	1 New Coat	2.00
William Keeble	2 Hats & 1 Hunting Shirt	.10
Eli Garner	2-1/2 Yrds. Jeans	2.30
William Keeble	Socks, Mittens, & Gallows	.35
William Keeble	About 2 # Lead	.20
William Keeble	1 Pr. Shoes & 1 Pr. "Scissors"	.25
William Keeble	1 Powder Gourd & Powder	.35
Joseph Counts	1 Lot of Shoe Thread	.05
A. H. Dunlap	1 Pr. Drawing Chains	.35
Peter Davis	1 Bu. Fresh Potatoes	.50
William Keeble	1 Rifle Gun	6.00
Eli Farmer	1 Pocket Book	.20

JOHN S. BOLING: A true and correct list of property sold by him as
Administrator of the Estate of Samuel Keeble, Deceased.

It would appear that William McCutcheon Keeble and Samuel Keeble, his
Uncle, were approximately the same size from the wearing clothes he
purchased. I cannot account for the date of this sale if Samuel died in 1869
as reported by Aunt Polly Keeble Helton.

HANNAH STAMPS KEEBLE DUNLAP

1805 – 1892

G.II   HANNAH STAMPS KEEBLE   JOSEPH ANDERSON DUNLAP

B: 3/12/1805   M: 10/14/1824   B: 2/12/1798
D: 1/6/1892   Blount Co. Tenn.   D: / /11857
                              Son of: Adam Dunlap, Jr. & Margaret Porter

II.   Children:
      James C. DUNLAP   B: @ 1826   M: Rutha Boling
      Adam H. DUNLAP   B: @ 1829   M:
      Joseph DUNLAP   B: @ 1832   M:
      Polly DUNLAP   B: @ 1835   M:
      Samuel P. DUNLAP   B: 11/27/1838   M: Sarah Caroline Davis
      Lorenzo DUNLAP   B: @ 1839   M:
      Hyrum DUNLAP   B: @ 1843 (twin)   M:
      Mary DUNLAP   B: @ 1843 (twin)   M:
      Rhoda DUNLAP   B: @ 1845   M:
      Jefferson DUNLAP   B: @ 1848   M: Nancy J. Davis

HANNAH STAMPS KEEBLE DUNLAP
March 12, 1805 – January 6, 1892

Hannah Keeble was the first female born to William and Mary Keeble. If one followed the tradition of the first girl child being named for her maternal grandmother, this Hannah "filled the bill." Her grandmother was indeed Hannah Stamps, daughter of Thomas Stamps, Jr., and Lydda (Lydia) Duncan Stamps.

Of the eleven children enumerated in her Mother's Bible, seven of the first eight were given only one name. The exception was Hannah, who was given the middle name STAMPS. Thus, we know for sure that she was named after her maternal grandmother. Her sisters, number nine through eleven, were also given middle names.

In the biography of Mary Keeble, mother of Hannah, I mentioned that Mary's grandmother married John O'Bannon after Thomas Stamps, Jr., died. In researching the O'Bannon name, I discovered that the Anglicization of the Irish name O'Bannon is WHITE. Perhaps this is the reason for some of the confusion regarding the engraving on the tombstone of Mary White Keeble's grave. In fact, as stated before, that tombstone should read MARY KEEBLE KEEBLE.

Mr. William H. Keeble, Professor at Randolph Macon College in Ashland, Virginia, wrote the following to me in a letter.

"I am wholly unable to account for my father's idea as to who William Keeble's second (wife) sic. Was; that is – to her background. He apparently always thought that her name was simply Mary White. If he ever knew that her name was Mary Keeble (prior to marriage) sic. he never mentioned it to me. But I have often heard him criticize himself severely for giving so little heed, when he was a youngster to the great store of family history that his father, Manly Keeble possessed."

Mr. Keeble's father was Pleasant Marion Keeble and this Civil War Veteran was responsible for placing the markers on the Keeble graves at the Keeble Cemetery and also the Walker Chapel Cemetery in Walland, Blount County, Tennessee.

To return to Hannah Stamps Keeble and her life, Hannah was apparently raised at the site of the Keeble Cabin near present-day Keeble Chapel. She was married to Joseph Anderson Dunlap on October 14, 1824, when she was nineteen years of age. Her husband was the son of Adam Dunlap, Jr. and Marjory Porter Dunlap. Her husband was born February 12, 1798.

I had asked Professor Keeble to describe Hannah for me, as he had known her personally. In his letter dated June 13, 1954, Mr. Keeble stated: "Aunt Hannah lived to a ripe old age. She was rather tall and looked as if she had been a very strong woman in her young days." She was the owner of the Bible I now have in my possession and the records I have given came from it (Mary Keeble's Bible).

In his letter of March 29, 1959, he gave the following description: "Now I will give you what I know about Hannah Keeble and her husband Joseph Dunlap and their descendants. I know nothing of Joseph Dunlap, but I knew Aunt Hannah right well."

"I was just about grown when Aunt Hannah died, but she was an interesting woman. She was rather large, angular, bony woman with a strong face and features. She was quite old when I knew her, in eighty, I think, but boasted of her ability to read even fine print without glasses. She was strong, self-reliant, and apparently always sure of herself. A good many of Hannah and Joseph's descendants were living in the upper end of Blount County when I was growing up. They were nearly all good singers and could jump higher and farther than any of the rest of us boys in the neighborhood.

Hannah's children were James Dunlap, Samuel Dunlap, Hayne Dunlap, and Caroline Dunlap. Hayne never married. Samuel married but I do not know who his wife was. I do not know how many children they had, but I remember one son, Samuel, who was rather indolent and had very little get up – didn't amount to much. I do not know of any other of Hannah and Joseph's children.

James Dunlap was usually known throughout the community as "James Crow." I do not know how he got the name "Crow." He was not very energetic or ambitious. He had several boys – James, Hayne, Hiram,

William, and John. I knew all these boys very well. They were all somewhat lacking in ambition but were very witty, droll, humorous, and all had un-usually keen minds. With enough ambition they could have made their mark in the world. They were all good singers, good dancers, good jumpers, but unfortunately none of them had any desire for an education. I could write a long story about them but I have said enough. The "Crow" boys gave a good deal of color to our community."

Mr. Jim Farmer, father of Clemmie Dunlap, wife of Charlie Dunlap, told me that James "Crow" got his nickname because of his long slim legs, was a good dancer, and especially liked to dance to the tune "Jump Jim Crow."

To continue with Professor Keeble's letter, "Caroline Dunlap never married but she had two sons, Hiram and Joseph. Years ago Joseph went west and almost disappeared from view. A few years ago, as an old man, he came back and visited his relatives. We have again lost track of him.

Hiram was a very industrious, capable, and ambitious young man and rather talented. He could have made a fine record in college, but the care and support of his mother made this impossible. He married my oldest sister. Hiram lived only three or four years after their marriage and died with tuberculosis. They, Hiram and Nallie, had two children. Estell died in infancy. Elizabeth is still living. She has one of the best minds I have ever known. She married James W. Davis and they are living in Sevier County in the Seymour neighborhood. Elizabeth was born October 6, 1893."

Mrs. Marian R. Dunlap, in a letter to me on April 19, 1989, states "One of the big mysteries in my Dunlap research has been WHO was Joseph Anderson Dunlap? James Dunlap named him in his Will-left him the farm he lived on-providing he "lifted" the note that James had signed with him-gave him a year to raise the funds in order to get that farm. There are some deeds back and forth and I think James may have bought some land from him (Joseph A.) to provide him with the money needed to pay off the note.

I believe Joseph A. and Hannah Stamps Keeble Dunlap named their second son Adam H., (after James' father, Adam, Jr.) although in the 1850 Census he is listed only as Adam, 21, Joseph, 18, Polly, 15, Samuel, 13, Lorenzo, 12, Hyram, 10, Mary, 7, Rhoda, 5, and Jefferson, 2.

Living next door is James, 23, and Rutha. There is a marriage for James Dunlap and Rutha Boling in Blount County Records. So adding this James to the list of Joseph A. & Hannah's household, I believe we have the complete family of Joseph A. and Hannah S. K. Dunlap." Hannah Dunlap's death date, as recorded in the Maryville, Tennessee, newspaper was January 6, 1892.

MANLY KEEBLE
B: 7/3/1807
D: 1/1/1882

Family record of Manly Keeble

Manly Keeble was born July
         3rd 1807

Rebecca Rhea Keeble was born
      Dec 13 1807.

Margaret Ann Keeble was born
      Dec 30 1830.

William Keeble I was born Oct 25
      1832.

Mary Keeble was born
      May 16 1834.

Sallie Keeble was born
      Sept 20 1836.

Katherin Walker Keeble was born
      Oct 10 1838.

John Harrison Keeble was born
      May 27 1841.

Samuel Keeble was born
      Dec 21 1842.

Pleasant Marion Keeble was
      born Sept 13 1845

Anderson Nurrin Keeble was
      born Jan 6th 1848.

A

Family record of Manly Keckle continue

Richard Henry Keckle was born
Sept 25 1851.

B

MANLY KEEBLE
1807 – 1882

The birth of Manly Keeble is recorded in his Mother's Bible as July 3, 1807. He was the fourth child of the union of William Keeble, Revolutionary War Veteran, and his wife, Mary KEEBLE. The spelling of his given name in the Bible is MANLY, although on several documents written throughout his life, the spelling is often Manley. Mr. Keeble apparently could not write his name, for most of the documents requiring his signature are signed with an "X" mark.

Manly was raised in the Keeble cabin, which was located across the road and down in a glen from the present-day Keeble Chapel and cemetery in the Walland area of Blount County, Tennessee. We know nothing of his childhood other than he had two older brothers, Thomas and Samuel, and an older sister, Hannah, to play with. There were seven children younger than he was.

In his father's application for a pension in 1829, William Keeble mentions that his older children have recently left home, and he is not able, because of his infirmities and age, to support himself or his remaining family. Thus we know that Manly and his older brothers carried much of the load in providing for the family while they lived at home.

No description of Manly has come down to us other than a narrative that has been told from one generation to the next – that four of the Keeble brothers together would have weighed over a thousand pounds. These four would have been Thomas, Samuel, MANLY, and Richard. Their other brother, Walter H., was described by his father in his application as a very sickly child.

When Manly was 22 years of age, he married Rebecca Rhea, daughter of Jesse Rhea and Margaret Blair Rhea. They were married on August 9, 1829, in Blount County, as recorded in Marriage Book O, Page 99.

Rebecca's father owned land in Blount County as early as 1801, although clear title was not obtainable until after 1806, when Tennessee, North Carolina, and the United States government made an agreement permitting landowners to title their lands.

Jesse Rhea was listed under Captain Montgomery's Company in the Early East Tennessee Taxpayers – Blount County.

Two years after Manly married Rebecca Rhea, his brother, Richard Keeble, married Rebecca's sister, Elizabeth Rhea, so that all their offspring were double first cousins. Sometime later in life, Jesse Rhea moved to Monroe County, for in a letter I received from W. H. Keeble, a grandson of Manly, he stated "The Rheas were residents of Monroe county, Tennessee, in the vicinity of Tellico Plains."

Mr. W. H. Keeble, in describing Rebecca, wife of Manly, "Rebecca was a rather short stoutish woman and it appears that all her children were on the short side, at least not tall, although the Keebles were a rather tall brood!"

Manly and Rebecca had the following children:

1. Margaret Ann – Born Dec. 30, 1830, who married the Rev. Pleasant Hugh Henry, son of Hugh Henry and Nancy Wheeler Henry. (She was a Henry prior to her marriage.)

2. William – Born and died October 25, 1832. Buried in Keeble Cemetery.

3. Mary (Pop) – Born May 15, 1834, who married Matthew B. Garner, son of Eli Garner and Elizabeth Rogers.

4. Sallie M. – Born September 20, 1836, and died February 14, 1850.

5. Catherine Walker – Born October 10, 1838, who married Jesse Cagle, son of George Cagle and Mary (Polly) Latham.

6. John Harrison – Born May 29, 1840 – 3rd Tenn. Cavalry Co. A. Drowned with the sinking of the steamboat Sultana on the Mississippi River April 27, 1865.

7. Samuel – Born December 22, 1842, who married Jane Garner, daughter of Eli Garner and Elizabeth Rogers.

8. Pleasant Marion – Born September 13, 1845, who married Elizabeth McTeer, daughter of James McTeer and Lovica Pitner.

9. Anderson Murrin Keeble – Born January 6, 1848, and died July 5, 1867. Buried in Keeble Cemetery.

10. William, age 1, in the 1850 Census. Not listed in the 1860 Census.

11. Richard Henry – Born March 5, 1852, who married Martha Ellen Stone, daughter of Joel Stone and Nancy W. Nipper.

In the Autobiography of Will A. McTeer, 1843-1925, Mr. McTeer relates the following: "Another means of getting together and having a good time was in singing school. The main singing master in our community was Manly Keeble. He taught The Old Harp of Columbia and had the whole book committed to memory from the gamet to the index. The youngsters went to learn some, but more especially to be together and enjoy themselves. When Keeble was not teaching they would assemble, especially on Sunday afternoons, at some neighbors and have a time of singing with one of their own members to "beat the time" and then the boys would go home with the girls."

For those of you who do not know, The Old Harp of Columbia (as described in the book) is a "system of musical notation with a note for each sound and a shape for each note. "Seven different shaped notes are used to represent the seven natural sounds of music."

Four part harmony was written in shaped notes in the book so that each part (soprano, alto, tenor, and bass) could follow their part and sing the tone according to the shape of their note. Usually the singers sing through the hymn or song using their Do, Re, Mis, and then they "launch" into the stanza of the hymn. The leader first gives the group of singers the "pitch" or key signature and then "beats" out the time, or sets the speed that the song will be sung.

I explain this method of singing to show that Mr. Keeble apparently not only had a favorable singing voice but also a good mind to retain not only the words of the hymns but also the notes that each section of the group should be singing as they harmonized. The greatest gift of all, in my estimation, was Manly's interest in the youth of the community and his willingness to take time to instruct the boys and girls of the community in singing. He must have been liked by the younger generation, as the singing school was purely a voluntary assemblage; and if Mr. Keeble had not had a good personality and tact in his relations with the children, they would not have attended the school and taken part.

W. H. Keeble, who I have quoted so often, stated in his letter of March 29, 1958, "I have often heard my father (Pleasant Marion) criticize himself severely for giving so little heed, when he was a youngster, to the great store of family history which his father, Manly Keeble possessed."

The 1850 Census for Blount County, Tennessee, lists the following persons in the Manly Keeble household: Manly, 35, Rebecca, 35, Margaret, 19, Mary, 16, Sally, 14, Katherine, 11, John H., 9, Samuel, 7, Pleasant, 5, Anderson, 2, John Clark, 5, William, 1. The Census lists both parents as having been born in Tennessee.

You will note that Mr. Keeble had a 5-year old boy named John Clark in his home at the time of the Census. I do not know the relationship between John Clark, son of a John Clark who made a trust deed.

Trust Deed - Record Book , Pg. 139 - Blount County, TN, May 24, 1858
I, Manly Keeble of Count of Blount, State of Tennessee, bargained and sold-transfer and convey to John Clark for consideration of one dollar to me in hand paid, and other considerations here-in after named, all my individual interest in a tract of land the William Keeble died seized and possessed of, lying in Blount County 14th District on the waters of Ellejoy Creek adjoining the land of Samuel Henry, Sr., Sam'l Henry (Denton) and others to have and to hold. The undivided interest in said land and to John Clark forever. I warrant him the title to said land and every part there-of in fee simple forever but this Deed is made to said John Clark as trustee to secure to Sam'l Henry, Sr., the sum of one hundred twelve dollars and fifty five cents due by note of land bearing a date with this deed which debts I wish to secure to the Samuel Henry, Sr., and deed to John Clark my un-divided interest in said land for that purpose.

Now, if I shall pay the debt and every part there-of in twelve months from this date then this not is to be void-but if I fail here-in, the trustee is to advertise said undivided interest in said land at three public places in the county and proceed to sell the undivided interest for ready money to the highest bidder without any reservation or redemption of any part. I hereby give up all benefit of redemption laws and trustee is to sell to the highest bidder and pay all debts, all cash and expenses and balance to me if any balance left.

Witness: His
H. J. Henry   Manly (X) Keeble
C. P. Tipton   Mark

In the 1860 Census for Blount County, living in the 14th District is a John Clark, age 45 listed as <u>Farmer</u> and <u>Sheriff</u>. Listed in this household are Priscilla, age 26, James 20, Benjamin 19, Adaline 17, Jane 15, <u>John 14</u>, and Elizabeth 12. It may be that the mother of the Clark Household was ill or died at the time of the 1850 Census so that John Clark, then the age of 5, went to stay or live with the Keebles. By 1860 the children were old enough for the Clark family to be re-united. This, of course, is a mere conjecture on my part, given the facts at hand.

Apparently Manly used the property as collateral for debts he incurred from the time he received the land from his fathers' estate.

Three years earlier than this above 1858 Trust Deed he became indebted to Samuel Yearout. Record Book Y Pg. 297 Blount County, Tennessee Nov. 25, 1855 "My entire interest 1/10th in a Tract in District 14 on the waters of Ellejoy Creek adjoining the lands of heirs of John Henry, Sam Henry, Sam Walker, Thomas Keeble, 186 Acres more or less-the above described land that on which William Keeble lived and died.

I am indebted to Clementine Saffell, Guardian of the Heirs of John Saffell Dec'd. in the sum of $60.00 and Mose Gamble is my security to her for the payment of same and I am desireous to secure him from any loss by my failing to pay the above mentioned sum.

This Deed shall be null and void if I am able to pay principle and interest. Yearout to sell land according to statute made and pay the above debt and interest and any overage to be paid to Manly Keeble.

                                                             His
Witness: C. Gillespy   Manly (X) Keeble
                 R. M. Saffell

Apparently Manly was able to pay off this note in 1855 so that he could again use the land for security in the later loan (1858).

It would appear that his notes were made prior to his even inheriting his share of the Keeble Estate for the transfer of the property from the Estate of William Keeble, Dec'd. to Manly and his brothers and sisters was not completed until 1860.

Record book 2 in the Blount County Clerks Office Pg. 575 dated Feb. 17, 1860 is the following document: We the heirs of William Keeble, Dec'd., Thomas, Samuel, MANLY, Richard, Walter H. for myself and Hannah Dunlap, formerly Hannah Keeble, and Soloman Farmer and Rebecca Farmer, his wife, formerly Rebecca Keeble and Stephen Davis and Mary Davis, his wife, formerly Mary Keeble and Jane Keeble, heirs of William Keeble, Dec'd. have this day bargained and sold and convey to Sam'l. W. Henry and Josias Gamble of County of Blount and State of Tennessee for the sum of $1,100.00 the receipt acknowledged-situa. County of Blount in the 14th Civil District on the waters of Ellejoy Creek and adjoining the lands of Sam'l Henry, the heirs of Sam'l. Walker, Dec'd., Thomas Keeble and others containing 187¼ Acres also another tract or parcel of land adjoining said tract just described bounded by Sam'l W. Henry, Thomas Keeble and others containing 33-3/4 Acres being part of the lands formerly owned by William Keeble, Dec'd. and being the same lands said William Keeble died seized and possessed of.

The 17th day of February 1860.

Thomas Keeble
Samuel Keeble
MANLY (X) Keeble
Richard (X) Keeble
Walter H. (X) Keeble

The 1860 Census for Blount County lists our subject as age 53.a Farmer with Real Property listed as $15,000.00 and Personal Property of $400.00. Still living in the 14th District. Others in the household at the time were: Rebecca, 52, Mary Keeble, Spinster, 24, Catherine, 21, John, 20, Sam, 17, Pleasant, 15, Anderson, 12, and Richard, 8.

Edgar "Si" Keeble, grandson of Manly, said that Manly was a spend thrift according to what he always heard and that the man had no business sense at all. When I showed "Si" the estimated value of Manly's holdings in 1860 Census, he was astonished.

Rebecca Rhea Keeble died March 4, 1864, which was near the end of the Civil War. She died about eleven months before her son, John Harrison, lost his life in the explosion and sinking of the steamboat "Sultana" on the Mississippi River near Memphis.

Two of her boys were on the ill-fated ship. John H. could swim and brother Pleas could not. John apparently, knowing he could swim, dove into the icy water and was probably pulled under by the hords of men fleeing the inferno. The two boys had been lying side by side on the deck trying to sleep when the blast occurred. Pleas, who could not swim, remained on the boat until he was able to find something buoyant to float on. Other men grabbed for his "raft," and he saw a dead horse floating by and so grabbed the mane of the horse and floated to land.

The men on this ship had been prisoners in the Southern Prison Camps and had been released to return to their homes. The ship was extremely overloaded with soldiers, horses, travelers, and produce. The railroad lines had been decimated in the war, and there was no other way to get home to East Tennessee but by boat.

The boilers on the ship had been repaired on the trip south on the Mississippi, but the ship owners were so greedy for profit that they would receive from the United States Government for transporting the troops home that they loaded on 2300 men when the capacity load was supposed to be something like 380.

The boat stopped at Memphis to discharge supplies and take on more freight and after dark started north on the muddy swollen river. Many passengers were scalded by the bursting of the boiler around mid-ship. Those in the front and rear of the ship had more time to attempt to get planks off the side of the upper decks for floatation items. The coal on board began to burn and the heat from the fire forced the men to jump into the water where many of them died. Pleas always regretted that he was not at home when his mother died.

He, in fact, was the last of the East Tennessee survivors of the Sultana disaster. The veterans who survived formed an organization and met each year until finally in the 1920s Pleas was the last survivor. The names of the lost were carved into a ship-like block of marble and placed in the Mt. Olive Cemetery in Knox County, Tennessee. Recently the descendants of the Sultana survivors have reorganized and meet annually in memory of their heroic ancestors.

Rebecca was buried in the Walker Chapel Cemetery in the Walland area of Blount County. There is a tombstone marking at her gravesite. The remaining sons kept the cemetery mowed and in good order until they could no longer handle the task. Walker Chapel was razed a number of years ago and the wood taken to the Walland Methodist Church for an addition to their structure. The cemetery on a hillside is now overgrown.

On August 18, 1864, Manly remarried in Knox County, Tennessee. His second wife was Rebecca Jane Murphye, born October 23, 1820. Her parents, as recorded in the Murphye Family Bible, were Malachi Murphye and Dorcas Dobkins. Rebecca died July 15, 1876. In the 1880 Census for Blount County, Manly was living in the home of his son, Pleasant Keeble.

It is probably at this time that Manly gave Pleasant Marion the gun that his father brought back home from the Revolutionary War. According to W. H. Keeble and Edgar "Si" Keeble, William Keeble picked up the gun on the Battlefield at Yorktown, Virginia, where he had seen the surrender of Lord Cornwallis. The gun was a smooth bore, flintlock shotgun. Pleasant Marion gave the gun to Edgar "Si" Keeble with the understanding that the gun should always go to a male descendant of the Keeble line. Edgar had no children so gave the gun to a nephew before he died.

Here is an interesting story about the gun. During the Civil War, Manly hid the gun in the hollow of a tree to keep either the northern or the southern soldiers from confiscating it. There were also renegades (outlaws) who, by their might or meanness, appropriated anything of value from the hapless citizens left at home.

After the war, the gun was retrieved from the hollow tree only to find that termites had eaten off the stock in the intervening years. Pleas had the gun restocked but unfortunately had the flintlock action removed and the gun "modernized" for the new era.

"Si" Keeble says that his grandfather Manly was a farmer all his life. He told one of the amusing stores that had come down from his father, Pleas. Manly believed in farming by the "signs." It didn't matter what the weather was like, the seeds had to be planted in the correct sign of the zodiac. Pleas was still living at home with his father at the time. The farm had some "bottom land," which is generally flat land that collects the topsoil when the river or streams overflow during the winter and spring seasons. Pleas worked up the ground for his father and then plowed the field, or laid off rows in both directions so that there were squares laid off to receive the seed corn. This particular day the sign was in the "bowels," and Manly strongly admonished his son for planting at that time, stating that he knew from experience that nothing would come up out of the ground.

Pleas, in order to placate his father, put an extra kernel of corn in each square to ensure that something would sprout in spite of the signs. The end result was that there was so much corn in the field that Manly was busy all summer working it.

Manly Keeble died January 1, 1882, and he and his second wife are interred in the Bethlehem Cemetery in Blount County.

REBECCA KEEBLE FARMER
1810 – 1881

Family Record of P. M. Keeble contin

Mary Estill Kieble was born
June 13 1886.
Died May 26 1875

Anna Rachel Keeble was born
Oct. 17 1889.

Edgar Rhea Keeble was born
Sept 25 1893.

Margaret Elizabeth C Dunlap
(granddaughter) was born
Oct. 1st 1893.

P. M. Keeble and
Margret E. McTeer
were Married Sept 22 1876

A   P. M. Keeble
Died March 4, 1931.

Family record of P. M. Keeble

Pleasant Marion Keeble was born
Sept 13 1846.

Margaret Elizabeth Keeble was born
Aug 17 1851.
Died Feb 17 1907.

Nellie Arizona Keeble was born
Oct 28 1871.

William Houston Keeble was born
May 7 1873

James Richard Keeble was born
July 17 1875.

John Edmund Keeble was born
Nov 7 1877.

Samuel Anderson Keeble was born
Aug 26 1877.
Died Apr 15 1893.

Andrew Elmer Keeble was born
Sept 11 1881

Nora Elizabeth Keeble was born
June 20 1884

REBECCA KEEBLE FARMER
1810 – 1881

Rebecca Keeble, daughter of William and Mary (Keeble) Keeble was born January 9, 1810, presumably at the home of her parents near present-day Keeble Chapel in the 14th District of Blount County, Tennessee. We know nothing of the childhood of Rebecca other than to say that she had three brothers and a sister older than she was and two brothers and four sisters younger than she.

On April 23rd, 1829, when Rebecca would have been 19 years of age her father appeared in open court in Blount County to make a claim for a pension as a result of his Revolutionary War service. The record was entered as a document into the June Session of the County Court records. In it William states that "Rebecca, age 19, Richard, age 18, Walter, age 13, Polly, age 10, Charlotte, age about 5 years, Jane, 4 years, and my wife are still living at home." He does not mention a younger sister Harriett born Feb. 13, 1813, whom we assume died in childhood.

On the 29th day of December 1829, Rebecca's father again returned to open court presumably to answer additional inquiries by the Secretary of the Department of War as to his proof of need for a pension. In this document, William describes in detail his losses in the year 1829 . . . among his possessions . . . "Three head of horses worth $25.00, one horse died the last of July 1829, six head of cattle worth $25.00, Two head of cattle died sometime the first of August 1829, three head of sheep, $3.00, fourteen head of hogs worth $8.50, three beds and furniture worth $30.00, farming utensils $8.00, kitchen furniture, one chest and one cupboard worth $12.00. I killed two small steers for the use of my family in the Fall of 1829, seven hogs died sometime in August 1829, one bed, my daughter married and took it away with her."

From the marriage records in the Blount County Courthouse, we know that Rebecca Keeble and Soloman Farmer were married on July 4, 1829. Soloman was the son of John Farmer and Elizabeth _____. Thus Rebecca moved from her childhood home and was given a bed and bedcovers when she departed. (Attached records say the marriage was July 23, 1829.)

We do not have a description of Rebecca's appearance. The three elderly members of the family that I questioned failed to describe her to me, although they knew her. It is interesting to note that in her father's Will, Rebecca is not mentioned specifically. Her unmarried sisters, Polly B, Charlotte W., and Jane H. Keeble, as they become of age, shall be furnished with "a bed containin 25 lbs. of good feathers and other furniture for said bed, in properties." This Will, written in 1834, left the bulk of the estate to his wife, Mary, for her lifetime, and be equally divided among her children upon her death.

From the Bible record of Rebecca Keeble and Soloman Farmer, by James Horton Davis of Murfreesboro, Tennessee, we learn the following:

Children:	(1)	William Farmer	born	January 11, 1834
	(2)	Houston Farmer	born	September 25, 1837 died August 29, 1856
	(3)	Joseph Farmer	born	January 6, 1838
	(4)	James Farmer	born	February 28, 1840
	(5)	Mary Farmer	born	January 10, 1842
	(6)	John Farmer	born	November 9, 1843
	(7)	Elizabeth Farmer	born	June 28, 1846

No. 1 - <u>William Farmer</u> married Mary E. Latham, Blount County, Tennessee, February 1, 1872, by Hugh Murrin, Justice of the Peace. William was a Captain, Company H, Third Tennessee Cavalry, Civil War. To quote Professor Keeble of Randolph Macon College, "Captain Bill Farmer was a born humorist and practical joker. He married a Latham and raised a large family, as nice and as upright a family of boys and girls as I have ever known. All very bright and all good singers. Tuberculosis got into the family and took away several of the boys. I was fond of the entire family as the older boys were about my age. All but one of his boys were teatotalizers. Capt. Bill Farmer was one of the best liked, most interesting, keenest minded men I ever knew. Children of this marriage were: John, Ola, Grace, Dellie, Loonie, Ida, Jim, Joseph, Huse, Charlie and Minnis." William Farmer died August 9, 1910 and wife, Mary E., died October 24, 1918. Both are buried in Bethlehem Cemetery, Blount County, Tennessee.

No. 2 - <u>Houston Farmer</u> did not marry and died August 29, 1856.

No. 3 - <u>Joseph Farmer</u> married Sarah A. Henry on June 20, 1861, in Blount County. He was a Private, 3rd Tennessee Cavalry, Company "H." He died in the Sultana boat explosion and fire on the Mississippi River April 27, 1865.

No. 4 - <u>James Farmer</u> married Ruena Jane Davis March 1, 1866, in Blount County. They moved to Walker County, Georgia, in approximately 1874. Two of their known offspring were Cora and Joseph H. Farmer. There were probably other children from this union.

No. 5 - <u>Mary Farmer</u> married James Davis. They also moved to Walker County, Georgia, at the same time James moved there. This connection is probably why James Horton Davis of Murfreesboro has Soloman and Rebecca Farmer's Bible.

No. 6 - <u>John Farmer</u>, Private, Company "A," 3rd Tennessee Cavalry, unmarried. He died with his brother Joseph on the Sultana April 27, 1865 (see attached declaration of Rebecca regarding John).

No. 7 - Elizabeth Farmer married Richard Keeble July 2, 1873, Blount County, Tennessee, the son of Walter H. Keeble and Mary (White) Keeble. There was one son, Walter Harrison Keeble, born in Blount County August 16, 1881. There are probably other children of this union. Historian Ruth Ritchie states that Richard and family also moved to Walker County, Georgia, and later to Dalton, Georgia, where he was employed by the railroad.

To return to Rebecca Farmer, mother of the above children, the 1840 Census of Blount County shows that Soloman Farmer and family were living in the 14th District of the county. There were three males under age 5 years (Joseph and James) and apparently a son who died young, one male 10-15 (William), Soloman, age 30-40, and a female (Rebecca), aged 30-40 years.

Rebecca's mother, Mary Keeble, died in 1855. In making her Will, Mary appointed Soloman Farmer as her Executor. In the Will, she bequeathed to Rebecca her "plain calico quilt." In the "Will Bin" at the Blount County Courthouse, among the final papers of Rebecca's mother's estate, was a paper stating that Soloman, as Executor, deemed it necessary and his duty to "make a trip to Paducah, Kentucky, to look after the legacy which he was informed and believed was coming to Mary's Estate from Charles Keeble, Dec'd." Soloman stated that he "started March 1st 1857 and came back March 12th, 1857 and spent the sum of $40.00. That he took the trip in good faith believing that it would be in the interest of the said Estate and the amount aforesaid was the amount that he was temporarily compelled to expend."

This was sworn to W. A. Walker, D.C. on December 2, 1857.

Charles Keeble, the deceased, was a brother of Mary Keeble and one of Rebecca's uncles.

Another document in the "Will Bin" stated: "Rec'd. of Soloman Farmer, Executor of the Estate of Mary Keeble, Dec'd. sixteen dollars the amount in full of the Legacy coming from R. Enders, Administrator of Charles Keeble, Dec'd. this April 22, 1868." Signed: Mary Murrin and attested by Andrew B. McTeer. Mary Murrin was a cousin of Rebecca's and a daughter of Charlotte (Keeble) and Andrew J. Murrin. This was her mother's share of the William Keeble estate.

The 1860 Census for Blount County, Tennessee, showed Soloman Farmer and Rebecca still living in the 14th District. Now Soloman is 54 years old, a farmer owning $3,000.00 in Real Property and $700.00 in Personal Property. Rebecca is now age 52. Children still at home are: William, age 26 with $150.00 in Personal Property, Joseph, age 24, with $150.00 in Personal Property, James, age 20, Mary, age 18, John, age 16, and Elizabeth, age 12. Rebecca Farmer died October 14, 1881. Soloman Farmer died January 14, 1886.

State of Tennessee   S.S.
County of Blount

On this 31st day of March 1874, before the undersigned authority, personally came Rebecca Farmer, who on being duly sworn by me according to law, depose and says that her age is 64 years, that she is a resident of the County of Blount and State of Tennessee, that her Post Office address is Eli joy Tennessee, and further stating says, that she is the wife of Soloman Farmer and mother of John Farmer who was Pvt. Co. "A", 3rd. Tenn. Cavalry, and who was lost on the Steamer Sultana on the 27th of April 1865 at the time said steamer blew up in the Miss. River, she also declares that her son, the said John Farmer had never been married, hence he left no wife, child or children, but he did leave parents who were dependant on him for their support, his father Soloman Farmer being past 67 years of age at this time and affiant past 64 years.

She now makes this application to the Office of Hon. Commissioner of Pensions for the U.S., Washington, D.C., for pension, as authorized to dependant mothers by Act of June 1866, and amendments there-to. Basing her claim for pension first on the fact of the death of her said Son in line of duty in the U.S. Service, secondly upon the fact that her husband, the said Soloman Farmer was too infirm to labor sufficient to take care of himself, and the affiant for years prior to her said sons entry into said service, August 1862 the said Soloman Farmer having been afflicted with Hernia of the left side previously there – to, as also an injury to the left leg, said leg being badly mashed by the turning over of a wagon upon which was loaded a saw log about the year 1860, hence the absolute dependence for Support upon their Son the said John Farmer, Dec'd. Pvt. Co. "A" 3rd. Tenn. Cavalry War of the late Rebellion. Whilst in said service said Son sent his father $150.00 for his fathers own use; Besides this Son, affiant had three other Sons in the U.S. Army during the late War of Rebellion, viz: William Farmer, Cap't. Co. "H" 3rd Tenn. Cavalry, Joseph, Pvt. 3rd Tenn. Cavalry and James Pvt. 6th Tenn. Vols. John and Joseph both being lost on the Sultana.

Affiant nominates and appoints A. J. Johnson of Knoxville, Tennessee, her true and lawful attorney to present and prosecute this application.

Test: J. W. Martin
      G. H. Felps

Her
Rebecca (X) Keeble
Mark

Subscribed and Sworn to before me by Rebecca Farmer, Claimant and by M. M. Irwin and A. T. Peery, her witness after the same had been duly read over to each of them and all of them, they understanding the same and I am not interested in this matter in anyway. This the 31st day of March 1874. J. A. Greer, Clerk.

Knoxville, Tennessee
March 26, 1877

Sir:

I have the honor to report in Case No. 214739 of Rebecca Farmer, Mother of John Farmer, late Pvt. Co. "A" 3rd Tenn. Cav. The applicant filed her declaration April 6, 1874 being her claim for pension, first on the fact of the death of her said son in line of duty. (Perished on board Steamship Sultana April 27, 1865.) Secondly on the fact that her husband (Soloman Farmer) was too infirm to labor sufficient to take care of himself and affiant for years prior to her son's enlistment in the service August 1862.

The evidence filed in support of the claim is of a reliable character, as will be seen from the Certificate of the Post Master at Maryville, Tennessee.

The Chief of the Widows Division referred the claim for investigation Oct. 15th, 1875, to determine merits of case-disability of husband during alleged dependence-Value of Property and Income during same period-Interest of Dr. Morton, family physician since 1858 and means of support of claimant and husband since 1865.

On the 12th inst. I proceeded by Rail to Maryville, Tenn. And made arrangements for conveyance to the Claimants neighborhood which was some thirteen miles south east of Maryville. But was advised that owing to recent rains it would be impossible for me to cross "Little River", there being no "ferry boats" on said river in the direction in which I wanted to go and was detained until the 15th, but in the meantime was taking evidence in the case of Sarah Bolinger.

The evidence taken shows that the claimant husband is not at this time an able bodied man which I find to be the result of his declining age more than anything else. I find him to be painfully afflicted with varicose veins, said to have been caused by a saw log falling on him about May 4th, 1860, which badly bruised and lacerated the muscles of the legs. His legs are covered with "lumps" from the size of a hens egg down to very small ones, I also find a very great tendency to indolence and almost total disregard for business of any kind. The evidence further shows that he was a stout able-bodied man prior to 1860 and that he was considered a stout man after he recovered from the afore said injury.

On the second point "Value of Property and Income during the period", I find that he owned prior to, and during the war, about 200 acres of land and a sufficiency of horse stock with which to cultivate it, besides cattle, sheep and hogs and apparently made a comfortable support before the war (Has no income but that derived from farming). According to the testimony the soldier was not 21 years of age when he enlisted (which I find to be true by the family record) and that he remained at home and worked on the farm and that his entire labor went to the support and maintenance of his parents prior to his enlistment, and further that he actually did contribute while in the service as will be seen from the affidavit of S. H. Henry. (See Ex. "E")

It appears from the evidence in the case that the husband and claimant had another son "James" who lived at home and worked at farming up to the time of his enlistment and who was at that time about 21 years of age, which is also verified by the family record, and it is further shown that he left home and enlisted about six months before said soldier (John) left.

On the third point, I find that the husband is indebted to Dr. Morton to the amount of about $60.00 for professional services before, during, and since the war.

The professional standing of Dr. Morton is certified by Dr. Jno. K. Blankenship, late Ex Surgeon for Blount County, Tenn. From the very best citizens of the County, I learned that Dr. Morton is in good standing as a man and as a physician. Under the circumstances it can hardly be presumed that he would stimulate his evidence or compromise his honor for the paltry sum of sixty dollars.

It would also appear from the evidence that the claimant and husband have had no means of support since 1865 but the rents or proceeds of their farm, their own energys, together with small contributions by their children.

I found the claimant and her husband living alone on a farm on which the husband first moved in 1811. They have no apparent means of support. There are a few old dilapidated out buildings near their residence, but not a beast of any description. (Though I learned from the family that they had one horse and one cow which was kept and taken care of by their son "James" who lived near the old residence.

A few facts in regard to the amount, nature and condition of their property may prove interesting in this case. They are as follows:

The husband was <u>always</u> involved and for a greater amount than the value of all the property he owned.

There was a Slave in the neighborhood-Alex Henry (See Ex. "C".) who had some facilities, and a considerable "tact" for making money before the war. His wife was always free and when Alex would accumulate a little money he would put it out at a large interest, and take notes in his wife's name.

About 1852 the claimant's husband borrowed about $100.00 from Alex and gave his note, and agreed to pay about 30 percent interest. Alex would occasionally loan him a little more money, add in the interest and take a new note. The matter went on in this way, still getting a little more money and renewing his note until the war closed at which time this indebtedness to Alex was in round numbers $1,800.00.

When the war closed, Alex informed Farmer that he wanted his money, and Farmer protested against paying such a high rate of interest. So they agreed to arbitrate the matter and the confree's decided to allow Alex just one half of his debt, or 50 cents on a dollar, and that the amount agreed upon should be paid upon the announcement of the decision of the arbitrators, Alex receiving only a small portion of the amount at the time, proceeded to collect the balance by Law, and to this end sued the said Farmer. About that time Farmer transferred his title to his farm to his son "James" for the purpose of (as is said) to secure the payment of the debt due Henry. Farmer said son "James" then executed his note to said Alex Henry for the balance of the debt and gives Andrew Peery and A. B. McTeer as Surety. And gave the "Deed in Trust" to said Peery and McTeer to secure them in endorsing his note. Andrew Peery then released said McTeer from the note and assumed all responsibility, with the express view, (I have no doubt) of paying the debt and getting the land for the debt.

Alex Henry has recently brought suit against the said "James" Farmer and his Securities and as Peery has released McTeer the payment of the debt will fall on Peery as he is the only responsible party, and neither the "Deed of Conveyance" from said Soloman Farmer to James Farmer or the "Deed in Trust" from said James to Peery is any account for the reason that just previous to this transaction the Legislature of the State of Tennessee passed a law by which a Deed, Title or Transfer of Land is nul and void unless signed by the wife of the husband transferring such real estate, but at the time of this transaction, such law, (As they say) was unknown to them. Consequently the title is in the claimant, and who has refused to transfer her title, and they have the same peaceful possession of it as they did before the war.

The main points to be considered in the settlement of this case area (in my opinion) as follows: The evidence shows that the claimants son James, had always lived at home and done for his father and mother up to the time of his enlistment, at which time he was about 21 years of age and had it not been for the war, would probably commenced doing for himself.

Again, it is a fact that the soldier (John) remained at home six months after said "James" had left and cultivated a crop on the farm with his father and for the use and benefit for his parents and that when he left home to join the army he went from the corn field and left his father standing in the field (as I am informed by the family) and as a matter of course the dependence devolved to a great extent upon their son John for whom the pension is claimed. Another and greater question to be considered is whether the claimants husband was, or was not, physically able to support himself and claimant by his own labor, and whether the proceeds of their farm would not have supported them without their own labor, upon which points I think the evidence is full and complete, clearly showing, that in either case, they were not dependent.

None of the witnesses (Except Dr. Morton) live at a greater distance than three miles from the claimant and they are perfectly familiar with their circumstances, and while there is some difference of opinion, as expressed in the testimony, I have no doubt but what each testified to what he believed to be the truth. As is natural the opinions of the neighbors differ as to dependence etc. but the evidence submitted is the very best character that can be obtained, pro or con, and I will further say that I could have proceeded with Exparte evidence and have made it either a good or bad case, but did not consider such to be my duty, and the evidence submitted compromises the sentiment of the neighborhood.

Very Respectfully,
O. N. Miller, Special Agent.

Hon. J. A. Benley, Commissioner of Pensions.
****

To the Commissioner of Pensions, I, Rebecca Farmer a pensioner under the pension certificate number 180472 hereby apply for the arrears due me under the Act of granting arrears of Pension approved January 25th 1879.

My Post Office address is Ellejoy in the County of Blount and State of Tenn.

	Her
James Donaldson	Rebecca (X) Farmer
James A. Davis	Mark

State of Tennessee, County of Blount. Signed in my presence by Rebecca Farmer who is known to me to be the person she describes herself to be and at the same time she exhibited to me her Pension Certificate which is numbered 180472.

Josias Gamble
Justice of the Peace for Blount County

****

Certificate #180472   Acts of January 25 & March 4, 1879

Brief for arrears of <u>Mother's</u> Pension

Name: Rebecca Farmer   Mother of:
Soldier: John Farmer   Rank: <u>Pvt.</u>
                                Company: <u>"A"</u>
                                Regiment: <u>3rd. Tenn. Cav.</u>

P. O. Address: <u>Ellejoy</u>   County: <u>Blount</u>   State: <u>Tennessee</u>

Date of soldiers discharge: <u>---</u>

Date Soldier Died: <u>April 27, 1865</u>   While <u>In</u> Service   Pension from May 20, 1875

Arrears of: $8.00 a month from April 28, 1865 to May 17, 1875

121

RICHARD PORTER KEEBLE
1811 - 1894

STATEMENT

Gamble, Tenn.,————————190—

M————————————————

IN ACCOUNT WITH E. G. KEEBLE,

Manufacturer of

ROLLER PROCESS FLOUR, BRAN AND MEAL

DEALER IN LUMBER.

MARION KEEBLE

MARTHA JANE KEEBLE

Marion Jee Keeble Was borned
July 9th 1840.
Martha Jane Keeble Was borned
April 16th 1844.
Elizabeth Jane Keeble Was borned
Sept 17 1866
Richard Parter Keeble Was borned August
th 6th 1868.
John Edison Keeble Was borned
August 11th 1869.
Margret Clementine Keeble Was Borned
March 8th 1871.
Edgar Gearg Keeble Was borned Aprile
th 1872
Matilda Elmonda Keeble Was borned
June 1st 1874.
Mary Ellie Keeble Was borned Oct
th 28th 1875
Marion Precilla Keeble Was borned
Sept 5th 1878
Henry Fitchus Keeble Was borned Oct.
28th 1880.

A

Marth Adaline Keeble Was borned
September the sept 21st 1882

Sina Gertrude Keeble Was borned
May the 3 1887

Rosa Lee Keeble Was borned Man
the 3o 1890.

Nancy ann. Keeble Was borned
Sep. the 29 18

1865

B

Marriages

Marian Keeble and
Martha Jane Clark
Was married December
21st 1864.

C

STATEMENT

Gamble, Tenn., _____ 190__

M_____ Seaths _____

IN ACCOUNT WITH **E. G. KEEBLE,**
Manufacturer of

ROLLER PROCESS FLOUR, BRAN AND MEAL
DEALER IN LUMBER.

Nancy ann Keeble departed this
life Sept 23rd 1865

Henry Feilden Keeble departed
this life Dec. the 3 1880

Marian Keeble departed this
life May this 5 1890

Rosa Lee Keeble departed this life June 30th 1890

Martha June Keeble departed
this life December the
22nd 1896

Richard Keeble departed
this life April 23 1894

D

Richard Porter Keeble
May 19, 1811 – April 23, 1894

Richard P. Keeble was the son of William Keeble, Revolutionary War Veteran, and his second wife, Mary (Keeble) Keeble. It is assumed, since he was born in Blount County, Tennessee, that his family was living on the land across the road and down in a glen from the present day site of the Keeble Chapel Church and graveyard in the Walland area of the county.

Richard was eighteen years of age in June of 1829 when his father made application for a veteran's pension. Undoubtedly he was assisting his father with the chores of the farm since his older brothers had already left the homeplace. When Richard was 20 years of age, he married Elizabeth Rhea. She was the daughter of Jesse Rhea and Margaret (Blair) Rhea in Blount County.

We do not know if the young couple remained on the Keeble farm to assist his ailing father or moved to quarters of their own. We do know that from Mr. Keeble's Declaration for the Southern Claims Commission, he moved to Millers Cove and lived there after January 1837.

"Si" (Edgar) Keeble of Knoxville thought that perhaps the farm in Millers Cove was acquired from some of Elizabeth Rhea's people in that her mother was a Blair. You will note that Eli Blair of Sevier County was one of Richard's witnesses in his declaration. We regret that Eli didn't mention his relationship to Elizabeth in his statement.

The original log cabin occupied by Richard and Elizabeth on their property was on the left side of Little River as you go upstream toward Townsend. Here they raised their two children, Margaret born in 1833 and Marion born in 1840.

Mr. Keeble had two farms, one containing 235 acres and the other about 175 acres. The second farm was probably acquired because of hard work and frugal living. While brother Manly appeared to have little business sense, Richard in contrast amassed an estate in his lifetime. Keeble owned land on both sides of Little River at the site of the homeplace. A story is told that he was plowing his "bottom" land across the river from the cabin when a storm raised the river into the plowed field. His 2-horse plow was in the field; and rather than have it washed away, he forded the river and carried the plow to higher ground alone.

In 1857 Richard's oldest brother, Thomas, felt it was his duty, as Executor of his father's estate, to go to Fauquier County, Virginia, in an attempt to ascertain what inheritance was due the heirs of William Keeble's parents per William's Will, which was filed in Blount County, Tennessee, in 1834. William's widow had died in 1855, and apparently Thomas now felt it was time to check into the inheritance from his grandparents.

Although there is no mention of it in Thomas's subsequent report, as Executor of his father's estate to the Blount County Court, I strongly suspect that the son of Richard Keeble, Marion, who would have been 17 years of age, accompanied his uncle Thomas on the trip to Virginia. In this way, the other heirs, Richard included, would know by someone other than Thomas what was learned of the family's inheritance.

Since the report of Thomas to the Court revealed that he found no inheritance, one assumes that Marion did not return home with Thomas but stayed in Virginia. In Richard's Declaration in 1878, he stated that son Marion went to Virginia in 1857 and did not return. (Where would a 17-year-old boy go in Virginia without a reason for going?) Did he find aunts or uncles there that suggested he stay? We have not a clue.

Further, Richard states in his Declaration that he did not see Marion again until he heard that his son was in the Confederate Army. Richard had a letter written to Marion suggesting that Marion was "at the wrong place and to come home." He stated that Marion was 25 years of age when he entered the Confederate Army, which would have been near the end of the war in 1865. It appears that Marion went AWOL in order to come home. (See the activities of Marion while in the Confederate Cavalry later in the book.) There is some discrepancy in dates at this time for Marion married Martha Jane Clark, daughter of John Clark and Matilda Thompson, on December 21, 1864, Blount County, Tennessee.

The war years are graphically portrayed in the Declaration that Richard Keeble sent to the Southern Claims Commission. He and Elizabeth had a difficult time protecting their property and crops and farm animals from confiscation and theft by the Confederate and Union Troops. One wonders if the spy glass mentioned being lent to Samuel Walker in his statement may have been an heirloom from the days when Keebles were sailors plying our eastern coastal waterways or crossing the ocean to England.

Marion and Martha Jane apparently moved in with Richard and Elizabeth and started their family – Elizabeth Jane (born in 1866), Richard P. (born 1868), John Ellison (born 1869), Margaret Clementine (born 1871), Edward George (born 1872), Matilda Clarinda (born 1874), and Mary Louiza (born 1875).

It was obvious that the old cabin was too small for all these children. In 1874 Richard and Marion started to build a new home. They moved upstream about 20 yards and went to work. They felled trees on their own land and worked on building when they weren't involved in farming activities.

In the spring of 1875, according to Matilda Clarinda, Little River flooded its banks to the highest level known, before or since. She told that the floodwaters were over four inches above the window sills of the new home under construction. She stated that her father and grandfather had not yet fashioned doors for the dwelling so that everything that had been moved or stored in the new house washed away in the flood waters moving through the house. The house was completed in 1876, and the family moved in. The house, or cabin, remained in place until the 1950s, when it was moved for highway construction.

Elizabeth Rhea Keeble had died in 1875, presumably prior to the family occupying the new residence. Only nine years after Elizabeth died, her daughter, Margaret, who had married the Reverend James Richard Coulter, died October 19, 1884. She left her husband and five children: Reverend Richard A. Coulter, William A. Coulter, Elizabeth Coulter, Nancy Jane, and James M. Coulter. She was buried in the Keeble Chapel Cemetery near her mother and grandparents.

Both Richard and Marion and his family continued to occupy the cabin until tragedy occurred in 1890. In May of that year, Marion died of Cholera; in December of the same year, Martha Jane, the mother, died of the same diagnosed illness.

In discussing these deaths with a doctor friend, I learned the following: "Inthrax," as listed on Marion's record, was Intestinal Diarrhea or what we now commonly call Amoebic Dysentery. He said it was quite common with Civil War soldiers. It was an infectious inflammatory disease of the colon, resulting in severe pain and diarrhea. The "Hepatic Disorder," also mentioned in the records, would follow right along with the Inthrax Fever diagnosis. The doctor then stated: "It probably was Cholera that was responsible for the deaths of both Marion and Martha Jane. They had no way of killing the infection at that time – you endured it for the remainder of your life. Cholera had the same symptoms as Amoebic Dysentery but was caused by a different bacterium."

It was the opinion of the doctor mentioned above that Martha Jane probably became infected with the same disorder through long-time contact with her infected husband.

The death of the parents left seven children under the age of twenty-one. Grandfather Richard, although almost eighty years of age, cared for the children. He became ill and Matilda Clarinda, only sixteen, cared for him to the end. He passed away April 23, 1894. His Will was written April 9th on his deathbed, and he rewarded Matilda Clarinda for her loving care those last days. Within two months, granddaughters Elizabeth Jane and Margaret Clementine married, the first to Robert Farmer, the second to Samuel Jackson Gamble. A newspaper clipping in the Maryville Times Wednesday, May 23, 1894, gave the following report: "Mr. Richard Keeble an aged gentleman of this place departed this life a short time since. He had been for many years a consistent member of the M.E. (Methodist Episcopal) Church."

My personal incite into the life of Richard Keeble was through conversations with Mr. Docie Keble and letters from W. H. Keeble, Professor of Physics, Randolph Macon College in Ashland, Virginia. This information was received over 35 years ago, and both gentlemen are now deceased.

Docie was born in 1892, so his knowledge of Richard was not firsthand. He attended every funeral, outing, reunion, or wedding involving Keebles. He was truly loyal to the family and thus was cognizant of many happenings and individuals in the family circle.

Docie said that Richard was a big, powerful man, large hands and feet – in fact large all over. He weighed approximately 240-250 pounds and didn't know his own strength. Although I can see no need for such a thing, with his farm animals and laborers, Docie said Richard could harness himself to a plow and with Betsy (Elizabeth) holding the plow handles, they could plow the garden. Docie also tells of Richard seeing a train locomotive off the tract and personally attempting to get it back on the rails. When it wouldn't budge, he backed off and said, "Humpf, that's the first thing that I ever tried to move and couldn't" (It sounded a little stupid to me, but Docie told it as it had been told to him.)

There were two Richard Keebles in the family at the time and to distinguish them apart in discussion, one was referred to as "Big Dick" and "Little Dick." Our Richard was "Big Dick," and according to Docie "Little Dick" moved to Georgia.

W. H. Keeble had met Richard personally. Let me quote from his letter. "Uncle Dick – My father tells many stories about his (Dick's) great strength. He was about six feet four inches, not fat but muscular and a giant in strength. According to my father he was regarded as the strongest man by far in the entire community. I saw him once when I was a young man in my late teens. He was then a very old man, probably in his eighties, and was still a giant of a man."

There is no doubt that Richard was a worker. The list of items taken by the federal and rebel troops shows the produce grown and harvested on his lands. Docie said Richard was considered "well off" financially by those of the Miller's Cove Community, and at one time he had as many as twelve mules and a number of slaves

The junction of Reed's Creek and Little River is the site where Richard assisted in raising the Union Flag, which the Confederate Leaders advised their troops to leave the flag alone. (The community was loyal to the Union.)

127

CIVIL WAR CLAIMS IN THE SOUTH

The U.S. Government created a Southern Claims Commission to consider claims of Pro-Union Southerners against the U.S. Government for damages or supplies taken without payment during the Civil War.

Richard Keeble was one of 75 Blount Countians who made a claim for his damages and in so doing had to answer questions relative to his losses. Much was to be learned of Mr. Keeble's station in life during the Civil War by reading the papers stored in Washington, D.C. relative to this period.

Richard Keeble   Claim #19,324 (This included 69 pages of information.)

All correspondence between Mr. Keeble's lawyers and the Commissioners in Washington, including a telegram from the Commission requesting that Will A. McTeer, Clerk of the Circuit Court in Maryville, Tennessee, take Mr. Keeble's declaration, are contained in the papers received from Washington. There were 80 questions to be answered by Mr. Keeble and 28 questions to be answer by the Claimant's witnesses.

The information garnered from this source is as follows:

On March 6, 1878, Mr. Keeble swore to the following: He was 66 years of age on May 19, 1877. He was living in Miller's Cove, Blount County, Tennessee, having resided there for 41 years this last January. His occupation was farming. He resided there at the outbreak and throughout the rebellion, and farming was his occupation the entire time. He was Pro-Union in sympathy from the beginning to the end of the War.

He fed many Union soldiers and gave word to his neighbors when he heard of rebel soldiers coming. He did not charge Union soldiers for the food he gave them. He joined a body of Unionist men in defending the parties who attempted to burn the bridge at Strawberry Plains, which was done under the direction of the U.S. Government. The bridge is in Jefferson County, Tennessee, and in the attempt Col. W. C. Pickens was severely wounded. As best he remembers, this was in the Spring of 1862. Elijah Hatcher, James Walker, Houston Walker, Aaron Burns, and, in fact near all of our Cove was on this trip.

Mr. Keeble had twelve (12) nephews in the Union Army.

"Of my sister Rebecca Farmer, there were four sons, William Farmer, Cap't., Co. "H," 3rd Tenn. Cavalry, Joseph Farmer, Private, Co. "H", 34rd Tenn. Cavalry, John Farmer, Co. "A," 3rd Tenn. Cav., and James Farmer, Private, Co. "A," 6th Tennessee Infantry. Of my brother Manley Keeble's sons: John Keeble, Co. "A," 3rd Tenn. Cav., Samuel Keeble, Co. "H," 3rd Tenn. Cav., and Pleasant Keeble, Co. "H," 3rd Tenn. Cav.

Of my brother Watson Keeble's sons (Author note – Walter Keeble was known as Watt - my assumption is that Will McTeer, Court Clerk, did not know Walter and assumed from the nickname Watt was short for Watson), three sons were engaged in the War – John, Samuel, and Richard, but their command is not now remembered. Of my sister Hannah Dunlap, two sons, James C. Dunlap, Pvt., Co. 3rd Tenn. Cav., Samuel Dunlap, Pvt. Co. "A," 3rd Tenn. Cav. Where and when they enlisted I cannot say. Mr. Keeble stated that he took sides with the Union and voted against secession every time. He was depressed at the news of the Battle of Bull Run or Manassas and rejoiced over the others.

"While the Rebels held this country, I had no one to go to for protection except my neighbors. I received no other than general favors, privileges or protection from the Union forces when they took possession of the country."

"Most of the men in my vicinity were gone-time of war. Elijah Hatcher, who is now dead, James Walker, now removed from here, and George Amerine, now dead, and myself were all old men and left here. We are in a little cove in the mountains to ourselves. The Rebels threatened several times to burn my property on account of my Union sentiments. At one time, I cannot remember the date, and being no scholar I kept no memoranda, it was in the winter, a party of Rebels came in sight of where and some black boys were at work. The black boys ran and the Rebels shot at us. They then came inquiring, who they were that ran. I told them and they declared that it was not so – that it was Union men I was harboring, and threatened to burn everything that I had. They went off, declaring that they would be back the next day at 12:00 O'clock and if these men did not come out they would then burn me out. While they were gone they killed old man Elijah Hatcher, as I was informed. I did not see him killed, but he was killed and they didn't come back anymore."

In answer to the questions, "Was any of your property taken by the Confederate Army?" Mr. Keeble had this to say. "Yes, At one time I had 17 fat hogs which I boasted was to give breakfast to "Lincoln's Men". When they came someone betrayed me and sent the Rebels who took them from me. I can't give the date but they were taken by Col. Toole's orders. He was Quartermaster at Maryville, Tenn. They paid me some confederate money for them but I cannot now state the amount.

At another time they took 8 beeves from me. I did not know what officer or soldier took them. I didn't ask them any questions. Sometime before, one of our citizens, a Union man was asking questions and making notes among the Rebel soldiers when they arrested him and kept him as a prisoner for some time, so I was afraid to ask too many questions. At another time they took the meat of 5 beeves. This was by Col. J. E. Toole. They fed and ate off me frequently. At another time they took 2 mules from me. I don't know certainly who took them but believe Dan Headrick was one of them. I never presented any account to the Confederate Government or any Rebel officer for them and never received any pay except as stated for the hogs."

To the question – Were you engaged in blockade running? Mr. Keeble stated: "I helped to blockage the Gap of the mountain against the Rebels."

To the question – Did you ever receive a pass from Rebel Authority? Mr. Keeble stated he received a pass to haul salt for his district and used the pass for that purpose – to haul the salt from Knoxville to his area. Date forgotten.

To the question – Had you any relatives in the Confederate Army? Mr. Keeble stated: "MY son, Marion Keeble was in the Confederate Army. He was about 25 years when he entered the service. At present he is living with me in Blount County, Tennessee. He left me when he was about seventeen years old and went to Virginia and entered the service there. I heard nothing from him from the time he left home until I heard from him in the Confederate Army. I had a letter written to him when I heard of his where-abouts asking him to come home and that he was at the wrong place, and he did so. I contributed nothing to his outfit or support."

Mr. Keeble said that he had never been in the service and believes he was above the age of conscription. He said that he was the owner and raised all the property that had been seized. It was taken from his farm in Miller's Cove, Blount County, Tennessee. He had 70-75 acres of cleared land and about 160 acres of mountain woodland, making about 235 acres in all. This was the home farm. He owned another tract of land situated in the 14th District of Blount County containing about 55-60 acres of cleared land and about 120 acres of woodlands. "My produce came from this last named place and was raised by me and my hands."

To the question – "Were you present when your property was taken?" "I saw it all taken. I sold them the oats, corn and bacon. The two mares were taken. The gray mare was the first taken by the Rebels and soon captured by the Federals-identified as mine and acknowledged by Gen. Burnside who promised to have the mare delivered to me or that I should be paid for her within 10 days. She was never delivered and I have received no pay." Some property was stolen at night but no claim is being made for it. "The army was camped on my place from Tuesday until Thursday night expecting an attack and said they wanted the provisions. The receipts were given to my attorney L. M. Blackman when I filed my claim."

To the question - Did you make any complaint? "I made complaint to Colonel Girard, whose regiment is forgotten, who was in command, stating that I had furnished what I could spare and the men were taking more, that I would rather give it to them than for the Rebels to take it, but I must have something left, when he furnished a guard which saved some of it, but the men continued to take things secretly.

To the question – Were there any vouchers given? "Receipts were given for these articles mentioned in this account and they told me to go to Knoxville and get my money, but when I went the authorities in Knoxville would not honor them: saving, that I ought to have got vouchers, but I hadn't so I got no money. The receipts were filed with Mr. Blackman."

"No payment has been made for any property charged to this claim. I did receive pay for some corn taken by Col. Buckner from Illinois-this was for a field of corn, 150 bushels for which I received $150.00, first getting a voucher and then at Knoxville got the money."

To the question – Was this property taken by troops which were camped in the vicinity? Mr. Keeble stated that the troops were encamped on his farm. They said they were expecting to be attacked."

"I saw the oats, corn, bacon and bay mare taken by the Federal soldiers and I saw the gray mare taken by the Rebels which was soon re-taken by the Federals identified and proven to be mine by Rev. Thos. Russell, when they promised to have it returned to me or the mare paid for."

"The oats were ripe and in the sheaf being packed up in the barn. The quantity taken was estimated by the officer himself who took the oats. They placed the price themselves and I suppose that was the market price at the time in U.S. money. It was taken on Feb. 1st 1864. It was Col. Girard's Regiment. Some of them said there was 10,000 men altogether, not all camping on my place, however, but all along down the river. There was a large number of horses, being a Cavalry Command and had a battery along with them. I can personally say there was a large army there. The men removed the oats from the barn themselves and a great deal fed on the spot, while some was carried in bunches off across the river.

The corn taken was husked and in the crib-but was not shelled. It was taken by the same group as the oats. Corn taken was 300 bushels, also estimated by the officer. It was good sound corn as good as anybody raises and the price they placed on it was $1.00 a bushel. The corn was fed on the spot and carried off in small loads in the same manner as the oats. No wagons were used to move the oats or corn.

The bacon taken was well cured and in the meat house. It was taken at the same time for the use of the men, and was weighed by one of the officers. I thought they told me there was 1717 pounds but it is given in this account as 1517 pounds. The price was placed at .10 cents a pound. It was good sound bacon. It was carried out into the camps by the men, and some eaten on the place.

The gray mare was a good large gray mare with glass eyes, 6 years old and a favorite animal. She was taken from me at my farm by Rebel soldiers and as they were endeavoring to escape and were captured by a party of Federal soldiers. Rev. Thomas Russell knew the animal, witnessed the capture and inquired where they had got the mare when they told him that they had gotten her from an old man named Keeble. She was taken to Knoxville and I, with James R. Colter, my son-in-law, went on to try to get the mare back-we found the command and an officer who knew the mare from the description given. My son-in-law, Jas. R. Colter, was personally acquainted with General Burnside-We learned one of the men had rode the mare to Bull's Gap and would be gone for ten days. General Burnside told my son-in-law that he would have the mare returned or have me paid for her. We went back a second time for her. But I never got either the mare or her paid for. I had been offered $150.00 for her and refused it so I think the price is fixed at $150.00. The mare was taken before Feb. 1st. 1864. Gen. Burnside said that the mare was necessary for the use of the army.

The bay mare was 7 years old, and a splendid large animal. She was taken by a federal soldier. He came once and tried to get her but failed on account of a guard that had been placed on my house. Some two or three weeks later, he and another man (or I took it to be the same man) with several others came near the house and stopped and after asking for the bay mare, took the mare. She was an excellent mare. She was worth $150.00 in U.S. Money. She was taken a short time after the oats, corn, and bacon."

Following Mr. Keeble's declaration are the declarations of witnesses John Gamble, Elizabeth Keeble, Samuel Walker, Thomas Walker, Eli Blair, and Jas. R. Colter.

"John Gamble states that he is 66 years of age residing in the 14th Civil District of Blount County, Tenn. which has been his place of residence since his birth except from 1842 to 1852. He is a farmer. He knew Mr. Keeble intimately as long as he can remember and resides within 3 or 4 miles of Mr. Keeble's home. They often visited each other daily and sometimes would not see each other for a month or more. He knew Mr. Keeble to be a Union sympathizer, and Mr. Keeble along with Gamble raised a Union flag in the gap of the mountain in the early part of the war, when times were beginning to get dangerous. Other neighbors of theirs were Josias Gamble, John Colter, Moses Gamble, Vance Walker. Will A. McTeer witnessed Mr. Gamble's signature.

Third witness was Elizabeth Keeble aged to be 64 next March (1879). She has been a resident of Miller's Cove for about forty years. Richard Keeble is her husband. She was present and saw all the afore-mentioned items taken."

"I mind I heard Mr. Keeble say there was over 1700 lbs. of bacon taken from our meat house. The gray mare was a good gentle, quiet animal. She was taken from our stable. The bay mare was a noble mare – was my riding mare. They came and asked if that mare was there. Mr. Keeble tried to keep them from taking her, but they went anyhow and they found she was fastened in the stable by a pole which they could not get loose- when they sent to the house to get an axe to cut the pole-when they did this a negro cut the pole and took her out."

John Gamble signed his name. Richard and Elizabeth Keeble made their marks.

"Samuel Walker, fourth witness, aged 55 last November, resides in Millers' Cove Blount County, Tennessee, has lived there about 36 years and is a farmer. He has known Mr. Keeble all his life. Their homes were about ½ mile apart. Both lived at the same places all during the war and since. They were together every day or two and lay together a number of nights, there is no telling how many. If they had written all they talked about-about the war-It couldn't be written down between this and Friday a week. I saw Mr. Keeble help put up the United States flag at the mouth of Reed's Creek in Little River Gap of the mountains as best I remember in the Spring of 1862. Then he, Mr. Keeble, with a large number of others went to help rescue some Union men who attempted to burn Strawberry Plains bridge (R. R. bridge) in 1862. He would not give up his gun when the Rebels tried to take them but got me to keep it for him. Other neighbors who can testify as to Mr. Keebles' loyalty are: James Walker, John Walker, James Taylor, John Taylor, Vance Walker and Spencer Walker. Mr. Walker states that he was at the flag raising and also assisted in the rescue attempt at Strawberry Plains bridge. "

"I went as a pilot for some spies of Col. Girard of the U.S. Army to spy out the Rebels in Wear's Cove and Mr. Keeble loaned them his spy glass. He also let the wives of soldiers in the U.S. Army have provisions and helped them all he could."

"Samuel Walker, fifth witness: Aged 31 last March, residence Miller's Cove, Blount County, Tennessee, was born and raised there."

134

"I was up on a hill opposite the Keeble house on the river and saw the soldiers taking hay and carrying bags filled, which I supposed was with corn. I did not see any bacon taken. They took it on down the road. They were temporarily camped there. I cannot say how much more was taken.

Thomas Walker made his mark Witnessed by G. C. Hutton and Wm. H. Nicely.

"Eli Blair, sixth witness, aged 56, resides in Sevier County, born and raised there."

"I was present and saw them taking the forage. I saw them taking oats and corn. Yes, I was myself a soldier, Commissary Sargeant Company "B" 2nd Tenn. Cavalry, and being home on furlough, went to Mr. Keebles. He told me that the soldiers were taking more than he could spare, where upon he and I went together to the Provost Marshall and made complaint, when it was stopped. I cannot now give the name of the officer, his regiment, or his rank, and do not know that I ever knew his name. He asked me if Mr. Keeble was a loyal man and I told him he was up to the time I went off, and I had heard nothing to the contrary since, where upon he sent a guard down with us.

The property was taken the 20th of January 1864. I may be a little mistaken as to the day but can tell near about the month. It was Sturge's Command. I think it was a Division-Col. James P. Brownlow 1st Tennessee Cavalry, Col. Wholford-Kentucky Calvary-Girard, Commanding Brigadeer division, Col. Brownlow told me himself, to tell my friends to hide anything they had and didn't want used, that the army was going to pass through the country and what they didn't use, they would destroy, that they wanted nothing left for Longstreet's Army, which was following. Then I saw a portion of this forage used. The corn was shucked and packed up in a crib in the ear. I would think there was 500 bushels or more. I only estimate the quantity by the size of the crib. It was large, fine corn that he kept for summer use."
Signed by Eli Blair and witnessed by Will A. McTeer

"James R. Colter, seventh witness: Age 47, Residence 14th Civil District of Blount County, Tennessee. Have resided in the District all my life. Was born and raised in the District-Occupation-Farmer. I am Mr. Keebles son-in-law."

Question – "If you know of anything of the Federal Soldiers taking and using the Gray Mare and appropriating the same to the use of the Army, please so state all you may know about it."

"Joe Hubanks of Wholford's Kentucky Cavalry told me, that there was a gray mare in their regiment that was Mr. Keeble's mare. He described the mare until I knew that it was the same mare from his description. Others of the same regiment told me the same. They told us where they were-the first time we went. They said they were going on a scout and the second time they said she was gone to Bull's Gap on another scout. These two trips were to Knoxville. Mr. Keeble and I went to see General Burnside who told us to come back in a short time and we should have the mare back again and if we did not get her he should be paid for her. We made two trips and each time called to see General Burnside who made a like reply to each occasion, but he never got her, neither was he paid for her."
  Signed by James R. Colter Witnessed by Will A. McTeer, Special Commissioner

The file contains a Petition stating Keeble lives near Gamble's Store in Blount County, Tennessee. He lists his claim as follows:

1 hundred and 10 (110) bushels of oats at 60 cents a bushel	$66.00
3 hundred bushels of corn (300) at 1.00 a bushel	300.00
Fifteen hundred seventeen (1517) pounds of bacon at .10 cents	151.70
1 Gray Mare 5 years old 15-3/4 hands high	150.00
1 Bay Mare 6 years old 16 hands high	150.00
	$817.70

"The Commission states that the property was furnished for the Army of the Ohio-Major General A. E. Burnside, and was taken by Elijah Cox, Sturge 1st Kentucky Cavalry USA and James Wilson Capt. & Q.M.

That receipts were given for the property, with the exception of the two Mares which receipts were placed in the hands of John Gamble, Esq. Of Gamble's Store Blount County, Tenn. To file with a claim before the Burnside Military Commission to audit claims in 1864 and said receipts were lost."

"The Summary Report awards Mr. Keeble $465.00."

For his 110 bushels of oats-		
$26.00 was disallowed and he was paid		$40.00
For his 300 bushels of corn-		
$100.00 was disallowed and he was paid		$200.00
For his 1517 lbs. of bacon-		
$51.70 was disallowed and he was paid		$100.00
For his Gray Mare-$150.00 was disallowed and he was paid		00.00
For the Bay Mare-$25.00 was disallowed and he was paid		$125.00
		465.00

Summary of the Commission

"Claimant swears to loyal sympathies and that he voted against separation. He aided and defended the Union bridge burners and assisted in raising a Union flag in the gap of the mountains in 1862. He had a number of nephews in the Union Army and a son in the Confederate Army. His witnesses confirm his statements and testify to his loyalty. He lived in Blount County in East Tennessee where there were a good many loyal men. He don't seem to have been complicated with the Rebellion and on the weight of the testimony we find him loyal. One mare which he said was captured from the Rebels cannot be allowed for the reason that the evidence is mere hear-say. For the other articles we allow $465.00."

WILL OF RICHARD PORTER KEEBLE OF BLOUNT COUNTY, ENNESSEE

Estate Book "F" Page 19   Blount County Tennessee April 1894

I, Richard Keeble, do make and publish this as my last Will and Testament.

1st: I direct that my funeral expenses and all my debts be paid as soon after my death as possible.

2nd: I give and bequeath to Clarinda Keeble one bed and $12.00 in cash and one cherry cupboard, two mohair dress patterns and to have her support out of my estate for twelve months and one side saddle. These gifts are made to her for waiting on me in my declining years, and through my sickness.

3rd: I give and bequeath to Watt Keeble five dollars out of my estate.

4th: I give and bequeath to Edward G. Keeble my two mares and my colt and one wagon and all my farming tools and my blacksmith tools and shotgun and fiddle.

5th: I now give and bequeath to all ten heirs of Marion Keeble a equal share in my estate after the heirs that have been specified hereto fore gets what I have bequeathed to them, them all share alike.

Lastly, I do hereby nominate and appoint Alvin S. Walker my Executor.

Signed this 9th day of April 1894.

His

Witness: William Walker Richard (X) Keeble
    W. T. Burns   Mark

May 1894 County Court:

Inventory of personal property of Richard Keeble, Dec'd.

1 set of blacksmith tools
1 set of farming tools
2 horses (Mares)
1 two year Colt
5 head of Cattle
15 head of Hogs
3 head of Sheep (in the mountains)
Lot of Corn (About 350 Bushels)
Lot of Wheat about 8 Bushels
Lot of Hay about 1200 lbs.
8 sides of bacon

2 hams and 75 lbs. Of Lard
1 Shotgun
1 Violin
2 Dining Tables
1 Walnut chest
Small lot of Books
10 Yards of Waterproof Cloth
3½ Yards of Broadcloth
2 Mohair Dress Patterns
1 Clock
1 Cane Mill and Pans
8 Gallons of Molasses
1 Sausage Mill
2 Wash Kettle
1 Brash (Brass ?) Kettle
1 Side Saddle

CREDIT

By Voucher:	#1	C. Phlanze receipt	$10.00 (Coffin) 8/3/1894
	#2	C. Phlanze	10.00 (Coffin) 12/6/1894
	#3	A. K. Hooper (Harper ?)	32.96 Items Purchased
	#4	W. C. Chumlea	8.75 Court Costs
	#5	C. T. Cates, Sr.	20.00 Legal Fees of Court
	#6	T. N. Brown	5.00 Legal Fees
	#7	J. H. Sherrill	18.50 Medical Treatment 1892
	#8	J. P. Blankenship M.D.	50.00 Medical Bill
	#9	J. M. Waters	4.60 Medical Services 1892
	#10	J. L. Martin	10.00
	#11	Andrew Hitch	83.00
	#12	R. M. Farmer	16.56 Services Rendered
	#13	W. C. Lance	5.76 Goods Bought
	#14	J. C. Gillespie	5.00 Hauling hogs to Knoxville
	#15	E. G. Keeble	6.75 Feeding Cattle
	#16	F. M. Webb	3.00
	#17	S. P. Rowan	10.00 Services Rendered
	#18	W. J. Hatcher	12.00 Willed Items

The following is a true correct list of sales made by A. S. Walker, Executor on the 12th Day of May 1894 of the personal property of Richard Keeble, Dec'd. This the 7th Day of July 1894.

Ben Cunningham, Clerk

ITEM	PURCHASER	HIGH BID
2 Beds	Priscilla Keeble	.50
1 Bed	John Keeble	2.60
1 Brass Kettle	E. G. Keeble	.70
1 Wash Pot	E. G. Keeble	.70
7 Chairs	E. G. Keeble	.60
1 Broad Axe	E. G. Keeble	.70
Set of Cups and Saucers	E. G. Keeble	.20
1 Side Bacon	E. G. Keeble	4.94
1 Side Bacon	E. G. Keeble	5.33
1 Side of Bacon	E. G. Keeble	3.00
1 Side of Bacon	E. G. Keeble	3.00
1 Side of Bacon	R. M. Farmer	5.72
1 Lot Scrap Meat	E. G. Keeble	.30
1 Pr. Sheep Shears	J. R. Davis	.30
500 Lbs. Hay	Rebecca Everett	1.85
500 Lbs. Hay	W. H. Davis	1.80
Lot of Hay	John Law	1.87½
3 Head Sheep	Lewis Huskey	2.85
10 Bushels of Corn	Isham Lail	4.10
10 Bushels of Corn	Isham Lail	4.80
15 Bushels of Corn	John Jackson	6.75
15 Bushels of Corn	H. H. Walker	6.90
40 Bushels of Corn	A. F. Burns	18.80
25 Bushels of Corn	A. F. Burns	11.75
10 Bushels of Corn	John Jackson	5.10
Lot of Corn	W. H. .Davis	20.62½
8 Bushels of Corn	R. M. Farmer	3.60
20 Bushels Corn	Thomas Jackson	7.00
10 Bushels Corn	Eliza Hatcher	3.60
20 Bushels Corn	Joseph Humphrey	7.60
20 Bushels of Corn	S. H. Ogle	7.20

10 Bushels of Corn	Elijah Hatcher	4.10
Lot of Corn	John Sloan	9.60
1 Red Heifer	E. G. Keeble	10.40
1 Red Heifer	E. G. Keeble	10.90
1 Brindle Heifer	E. G. Keeble	5.80
1 Black Steer	E. G. Keeble	8.00
1 Small Red Steer	E. G. Keeble	5.20
1 Spotted Sow	E. G. Keeble	7.20
1 Black Sow	E. G. Keeble	5.20
13 Head of Shotes	E. G. Keeble	32.23
1 Truss	C. J. Garland	.15

****

Additional Inventory of Assets of Richard Keeble, Dec'd. Estate book "F," Page 172.

ITEM	PURCHASER	HIGH BID
Wheat - 15½ Bushels	sold for:	7.75
Harness Leather	sold for:	2.00
Small Lot of Oats	sold for:	1.55
Harness Leather (5½ lbs.)		1.31
Corn, 22½ Bushels		11.85
Rec'd from W. C. Chumlea C&M		46.12
To Amt. Of Listed Sales		260.41
Rec'd. on J. L. Martin Note		25.24
Reported this Date		70.58
Interest on Sale Notes		8.83
TOTAL		$364.56

****

In Estate Book "K," Page 32, August 1894, a list of the sale of personal property was itemized by A. S. Walker, Executor of Richard Keeble, Dec'd. Estate (continued)

3½ Yards of Broadcloth	E. G. Keeble	5.25
3⅓ Yards of Waterproof Cloth	E. G. Keeble	1.60
3⅓ Yards of Waterproof Cloth	E. G. Keeble	1.70
1 Piece of Waterproof Cloth	Lewis Huskey	.55
3½ Yards of Waterproof Cloth	R. M. Farmer	2.60

3⅓ Yards of Waterproof Cloth	E. G. Keeble	2.05
1 Chest	E. G. Keeble	.50
1 Chest	J. E. Keeble	.80
1 Clock	E. G. Keeble	.10
1 Sausage Mill	James Headrick	.35
1 Glass & Book	J. E. Keeble	.05
1 Book	R. N. Farmer	.50
1 Churn	Clarinda Keeble	.40
2 Tables	E. G. Keeble	.15

After the sale of the personal property, there was a partial settlement made to the heirs of the Estate May 12, 1894.

In Estate Book "F," Pages 32 and 33, these partial settlements were listed.

John E. Keeble	$1.70
E. G. Keeble	1.70
R. P. Keeble	1.70
Margaret C. Gamble	1.70
Mary L. Farmer	1.70
Bettie J. Farmer	1.70
M. C. Hatcher	1.70
M. P. Graves	1.70
Sine G. Keeble	1.70
Martha A. Keeble	1.70

****

E. G. KEEBLE et al. VS: R. P. KEEBLE et als.
Estate consists of two tracts of land: 1 tract situated in the 14th Civil District known as the Richard Keeble's "Moses Gamble" Tract or farm containing 100 Acres more or less adjoining on the North the land of Moses Gamble, on the East the land of Nick Brewer, on the South the lands of Wallace Millsaps, and on the West by "Busher" Gamble.

The other tract known as "Richard Keebles Knob Tract" situated in the 14th District of Blount County bounded by lands of William Hill in the East, lands of James Farmer in the North, the "Cowan Lands" on the West and South by lands of Reece Davis containing 80 Acres more or less.

Sale as advertised sold October 6, 1894. John White bought the 100 Acre Tract for $350.00. Robert M. & Joe H. Farmer bought the 80 Acre (Knob Tract.) for $445.00. The latter men had George C. Davis as their Surety.

****

MINUTE BOOK 18 NOVEMBER 1894 PAGE 56
ED. G. KEEBLE et al VS: MATILDA C. KEEBLE et als:
Four of the ten heirs have sold their portion of land to E. G. Keeble so that he owns half interest. Matilda C., Martha A., Marion P., Sina G., and Mary L. Farmer are each owners of one tenth.

Depositions of John D. Headrick and E. Goddard state the lands so situated that they cannot be partitioned in kind. Clerk to advertise sale of land for twenty days by printed posters at five public places in Blount County-one at Courthouse door, one at voting place in 18th District, one at Henry's or Neubert's Mill and Courthouse Door in Knoxville. Tract in 18th District (Formerly the 15th District) in Miller's Cove on Little River known as Richard Keeble Home Farm and fifteen Acre tract known as the Fry Tract platted separately. Sold the 14th Day of December 1894 Pg. 120. Sold to E. G. Keeble for $2800.00. These plots are divided by Little River and lie below Hatcher Ford containing 264 Acres. The Fry Tract of 15 Acres was sold to V. B. Walker for $37.00.

It should be recorded that all the settlements of Richard Keeble Estate had to be handled through the Circuit Court since at least five of the heirs were minors: Namely, Sine G. Keeble, Martha A. Keeble, Marion P. Keeble, Mary L. Keeble, and Clarinda Keeble.

Apparently the Chancellor of Circuit Court appointed John M. Snider, Guardian of these minor children and he distributed the shares of the Estate to the Minors. However, prior to the final settlement of the Estate, Edward G. Keeble became Guardian on May 28, 1894.

In the Lawsuit-E. G. KEEBLE VS: R. P. KEEBLE et al. Two tracts of land were sold October 6, 1894 and the shares were distributed to the ten heirs on October 6, 1895. Each of the heirs received $73.27.

In the Lawsuit-ED. G. KEEBLE VS: MATILDA C. KEEBLE et al. Land was sold for partition Dec. 14, 1894. Homestead tract to Ed. G. Keeble for $2800.00.

Since E. G. Keeble had bought out four of the heirs on the Homestead Tract, payments were made to the heirs as follows:

E. G. Keeble	$1302.55
Matilda C. Keeble	260.51
Martha A. Keeble	260.51
Marion P. Keeble	260.51
Sine G. Keeble	260.51
Mary L. Farmer	260.51
Distribution of the "Fry Lot"	38.66
E. G. Keeble	3.86
John E. Keeble	3.86
M. E. Keeble	3.86
M. L. Keeble	3.86
M. P. Keeble	3.86
M. A. Keeble	3.86
S. G. Keeble	3.86
R. P. Keeble	3.86
Bettie Farmer	3.86
M. C. Gamble	3.86

HARRIET KEEBLE
2/13/1813 –

HARRIET KEEBLE

According to the Bible record of Mary Keeble, a daughter, Harriet Keeble was born to William Keeble, Revolutionary War Veteran, and his wife, Mary, on February 13, 1813. One would assume that this child was named in honor of Mary's sister, Harriet, who died sometime shortly after the birth of this Harriet.

The aunt, Harriet, was living when Richard Keeble wrote his Will in 1811. However, in Will Book 14, November 21, 1816, in Fauquier County, Virginia Harriet apparently was dying, for she left her rights to her father's Estate to "her loving Mother Hannah Keeble-and at Hannahs' death those Rights were to be equally divided between sister Mary and her two brothers-Thomas and Charles G. Keeble, and her niece Eliza White."

Mr. William Keeble did not mention his children by name in 1818 when he first applied for a pension from the federal government. The 1810 Census for Tennessee was destroyed, and so that source of information is non-existent. However, when Veteran Keeble wrote to the government attempting to reinstate his pension in 1829, he mentioned his children living at home. The list included Rebecca, age 19, Richard 18, Walter 13, Polly 10, Charlotte 5, and Jane 4 years of age. Harriet, who would have been about sixteen years, is not mentioned.

Thus, I assume that Harriet had died either at birth or at sometime in her early childhood. No mention of her is made from any other source than from the Bible. She is not listed as an heir to either real or personal property in the Wills of her Father (1834) or her Mother (1855). The older members of the family that I interrogated had no knowledge of this Harriet Keeble at all.

WALTER HARRISON KEEBLE
11/14/1815 – 4/25/1897

BIRTHS

William Keeble Was Borned
May 20th 1837

John Keeble was Borned
August 20th 1838

Nancy Keeble was Borned
August 22nd 1840

Samuel Keeble Was Borned
April 12th 1843

Mary Keeble was Borned
October 24th 1845

Richard Keeble was Borned
February 14th 1849

Jane Keeble was Borned
September 5th 1853

BIRTHS

Amey Keeble was borned August the 28, 1840

Stephen Keeble was borned May the 16, 1880

Faye Keeble the wife of Steve Keeble was
Borned May the 5, 1884.

Annas Keeble born Nov. 13, 1902

Vala Keeble Borned Jan 28, 1905,

Cecil Keeble Borned Dec. 25, 1907,

Cara Keeble Borned April, 23, 1911,

Tsa Keeble Borned Jan. 13, 1914,

Hazel B. Keeble " Oct. 4 1917,

Roy Keeble Borned June 21, 1919

Cara Keeble was Borned the 23
day of April 1911

Junior Keeble Borned May 27, 1924,

Junior 27/1924

B

MARRIAGES

Steve Keeble was married
December the 8, 1901

Nancy Keeble born August
the 11, 1913
Jane Keeble die August
the 18, 1913
Pup Keeble die February
the 14, 1915 -

Hazel Beatrice Keeble was
born October the 14 1917
Died January the 2 1918

Guy Keeble was born June 21
1919

Cora Keeble and Willie B. Johnson.
April 5 1911 n.

Roy Keeble and Louise Singer
C 6 1913

Barbara T Alexander

Kyle Hatcher Nov 1 1928 May 16, 1931

Ray Hatcher August 7, 1944

L. C. Keeble Dec. 19, 1940

Keneth Keeble July 2 1, 1942

Dallas Leon Keeble

Roy Lynn Keeble (Born + Died) Sept 2 7, 1940

Billie Ray Keeble (Dec. 4, 1941)

(Died March 9 1942)

Wynetta Keeble aug

Vernon Dewayne dec 1945

Wanda Sue Keeble dec 1947

Larry Keeble april 25 1948

Judith Faye Keble Oct. 10 1957

Don Eugene Keeble

D

DEATHS

Loyl Keeble died September 15, 1937 Wensday

Annas Keeble was borned november the 13, 1902 dide December the 22 1902

James Dyer dide march the 20 1916

Walter Keeble Died Aprile 25 1934

Pheba Anne Dyer died January 5 1897

Little Annas Keeble was borned november the 13, 1902 and dide December the 22 in the year 1902.

Maneg Skeeble Died August the M. 19, 13

Jane keeble dide august th 18, 1913

Junior Keeble Wensday nov. 7, 1942

Billie Kay Keeble died march 9th 1942

Barbara J Alexander was born
May 16, 1931 at Meadow _____

Kyle Hatcher was born Nov 1, 1928

Junior Hatcher

Ray Hatcher — aug 7, 1942
was Barned May the 27,

Loy Keeble died at the age of 58 ___
4 month 10 day old.

Ben Alexander and Ida Keeble ___
Married July 4, 1930

Loy Keeble Died Wenesday Sep. 15, 1937,

Annas. Keeble Died Dec 22, 1902,

Hazel Keeble Barned Oct, 14, 1917,
        Died Jan, 2nd 1918,

Junior Keeble died November 18, 1942

F

WALTER HARRISON KEEBLE
November 14, 1815 – April 25, 1897

The page upon which Walter Harrison Keeble's name should appear in his mother's family Bible has deteriorated to such an extent that his name is not legible at all. We do know that it once was listed in that his birth date remains below the missing name. Our subject was known to the family members as Watt, and to those of the older generation whom I had an acquaintance, he was called Uncle Watt.

Except for the gravestone markers that once stood facing the parking lot at Cloyds Creek Cemetery, we would not have known the death date of Walter or the birth and dead dates of his wife Mary (Polly) White Keeble. Since the stones were so similar to those in the Keeble Cemetery, one would suppose Pleasant Marion Keeble had them erected also. Those stones have disappeared from the Cloyds Creek Cemetery.

William's first mention of his son, Walter, was in his declaration of April 1829 in his attempt to get his pension reinstated. In the Declaration he states that Walter is still living at home, is thirteen years of age, and is very sickly. In a second Declaration written in December 1829, he gives us a little more information about Walter's condition. Besides being sickly, he "has a wen on his chest." The dictionary defines a "wen" as a cyst formed by blocking of a skin gland and filled with fatty material.

Walter must have outgrown some of his childhood weaknesses, for in his father's Will written in 1834, William states that he wants his wife, Mary, to have all he possess, with the condition that Walter is to have the 75 acres of land, yet undeeded, and additionally a colt, and a yoke of oxen, with the understanding that he remain on the farm and care for his mother for two years. The oxen are given with the understanding that they will be available for use on the homeplace for four years after William's death.

It would appear that Walter fulfilled his father's wishes in staying on the farm and caring for his mother for two years. He then received his Deed for his 25 acres and married Mary White on August 15, 1836, in Blount County. We do not know if this Mary White was a kin of Charlotte and Wilson White.

Children of this union were William, John, Nancy, Samuel, Mary, Richard, and Jane. The names are almost identical with Walter's brothers and sister's names.

In the early days of my search into the Keeble family, Aunt Polly Helton said that Walter and Mary had lived in their community but had moved to Georgia, and she had never heard of them further. One wonders if perhaps Walter and family did move to Georgia when there was quite a migration to Walker County from Blount County, Tennessee, then perhaps returned to Blount County, settling in the lower section of the County near the Friendsville area.

Aunt Polly's family moved to Sevier County, so the distance was too great for much visiting back and forth. Walter was a farmer.

MARY BANKS (POLLY) KEEBLE DAVIS
12/14/1817 -

MARY BANKS KEEBLE DAVIS

Mary Banks Keeble was born December 14, 1817, according to the record in her mother's Bible, the ninth of eleven children of William Keeble, Revolutionary War Veteran and his wife, Mary (Keeble) Keeble. I do not know the derivation of the middle name BANKS; the mother had named one of her children Hanna STAMPS in honor of her mother, who had been born a Stamps. I can think of no member of the family who married a Banks or even a neighbor in the community so named.

We know nothing of Mary's childhood other than to say that William, her father, mentioned her in a Declaration for renewal of his pension, saying that Polly Keeble, aged 10, along with the younger children of the family, still lived at home. Actually Polly would have been eleven years old at that time (1829).

Polly was seventeen years old in 1834 when her father died. She was specifically mentioned in his Will. "It is my Will that Polly B. Keeble . . . as she becomes of age shall be furnished with a bed containing 25 lbs. of good feathers and furniture for said bed in properties."

Apparently Polly remained in the homestead with her mother. She married Stephen Davis in Blount County on April 5, 1838. She was twenty years old at the time of her marriage.

Stephen Davis' parents were Thomas Davis and Sarah (Sary) Mize Davis. Their marriage date is recorded in Wilkes County, North Carolina, in 1817. The father's name appears on the records of the Millers Cove Missionary Baptist Church in 1820. The father had received two Land Grants for acreage on Hesses' Creek in Millers Cove of Blount County, Tennessee, so their property was not far from the Keebles.

The 1860 Census lists Stephen as being 42, the same age as Polly. The Census lists the head of the household as "Jane Keeble, Tenant." Apparently when the homeplace was sold to Walter Keeble by his brothers and sisters in August of 1855, he permitted Jane, Stephen, Mary, and their children to live on there.

The 1860 Census enumerates the children of Stephen and Polly as Charlotte, Eliza (Elijah), Jane, Mary, Sarah, William, Rebecca, and Walter.

Since I can find no information on the Davis family after 1860, I surmise the family left the area just prior to the Civil War. The Mormon Library in Salt Lake City has information on some of Stephen and Mary's children and gave us the address of the person submitting the information. Our queries sent to the Davis descendants have gone unanswered. We will continue to seek information about this family.

DEED BOOK X, Pg. 326

This indenture made and entered into the 24th day of January 1850 between Stephen Davis and his wife Mary formerly Mary Keeble of the one part and Walter H. Keeble of the other part., both of the County of Blount and State of Tennessee. Witness that the said Davis and wife for and in consideration of the sum of twenty-four dollars and fifty cents sell to Walter H. Keeble a certain tract or undivided interest, it being the ninth part of a tract of land Granted by the State of Tennessee to William Keeble known as the tract of land on which said William Keeble last lived before his death. (Twenty four and one half acres.)

Stephen Davis

Her
Mary (X) Davis
Mark

In August 13, 1855 Walter H. Keeble bought the shares of:
Soloman and Rebecca Farmer
Jane H. Keeble
Joseph and Hannah Dunlap

CHARLOTTE WHITE KEEBLE
5/21/1819 – 10/9/1847

CHARLOTTE WHITE KEEBLE

Charlotte White Keeble was born May 21, 1819, the daughter of William Keeble, Revolutionary War Veteran, and his wife, Mary. This birth is recorded in Mary's Bible. One must assume that Charlotte was raised in the cabin home near the present Keeble Chapel in the Walland Community of Blount County, Tennessee.

Apparently she was named for her deceased aunt, Charlotte Keeble White, sister of her mother. Charlotte, the aunt, had married Wilson White in Fauquier County, Virginia, in 1802 and then came to Blount County where she resided near the Keeble home for the remainder of her life. Her father, Richard, in his Will written in 1811, mentions that daughter Charlotte is deceased.

Charlotte White Keeble, our subject, was the next to the youngest of the eleven Keeble children, so one would assume that she had the loving care of not only her parents but several of her older brothers and sisters in the household.

We know nothing of her childhood and doubt that she, or the other children, had any formal education, as almost all of them signed documents later in life with an "X" mark witnessed by those who could write.

On August 27, 1844, Charlotte married Andrew J. Murrin, son of Robert Murrin and Catherine _____ of Blount County.

We know that the Keeble family apparently held Andrew in high esteem, for a good many of the legal documents obtained by the Keeble family bore the signature of Mr. Murrin as a witness to their "Xs." We know from the tombstone marker at her grave in Keeble Cemetery, erected by Pleasant Marion Keeble, that Charlotte lived only three years after marriage. One might surmise that she may have died from complications in childbirth or from tuberculosis. We have no proof of the cause of death. She died years before our family sources were born, so no one knew of her life's story.

In the "Will Bin" at the Blount County Clerk's Office, there is an envelope titled A. J. MURRIN. It contains the following petition:

"State of Tennessee, Blount County: to S. J. McReynolds, County Judge:

"State of Tennessee, Blount County: to S. J. McReynolds, County Judge: Your petitioner, A. J. Murrin would represent to your Honor that he wishes to be appointed Guardian to his minor daughter named Mary Murrin who had not attained the age of 14 years this 2nd. Of December 1857. Signed: A. J. Murrin.

Witnesses to the signature were: William Davis and M. C. Kounts.

With the marriage of Andrew and Charlotte in 1844, daughter Mary would have been about 12 or 13 years of age in 1857.

I would assume that Mary's father was declared her guardian so that Mary could inherit that share of her grandmother's (Mary Keeble) estate, the part that would have passed to her mother, Charlotte, had she lived. The grandmother died in 1855.

In this same envelope are notations that A. J. Murrin had died by the year 1874 and that Mary Murrin was named the Administrix of his estate. The date on A. J. Murrin's tombstone at Keeble Chapel states he died Januay 31, 1868. It is my opinion that date is in error.

We do know that A. J. Murrin and Richard Keeble purchased the Keeble Graveyard from Samuel W. Henry for $5.00 on October 25, 1867, this graveyard having been established on the part of the original William Keeble Land Grant. It was sold by the Keeble heirs following the death of their mother without a thought of protecting the burial place of their parents. The sale was recorded in the Register of Deeds office, Blount County Courthouse the 11th of November 1867. R. E. Tedford, Registrar.

Mary Murrin, daughter of A. J. Murrin and Charlotte Keeble Murrin, signed for a $16.00 inheritance from the estate of her Uncle Charles Keeble of Paducah, Kentucky, on April 22, 1868. This document was in the Will Bin with the other described papers.

Another document in the envelope mentioned above reads: "Blount County, Tenn. We, Mary Martin, A. H. Dunlap and Alex Eagleton are firmly bound to the State of Tennessee with the penalty of $1,000.00. Signed the 9th of January 1874. The identification on the front of the document reads: Mary Murrin Appt'd Admx. Of A. J. Murrin, Dec'd."

There is a marriage record filed in Blount County for a Mary Murrin who married one Jacob H. Harman on March 10, 1875. The 1880 Census for Blount County lists a Jacob Harman with wife Mary and a child, William E. Harman. I do not know if this is the Mary Murrin above, but the dates would seem to be in line.

Also listed on the above envelope from the County Clerk's Office someone had written that A. J. Murrin was deceased by 1874 and another notation that Mary herself was deceased by 1879. (Mary would not have been listed in the 1880 Census if she had died in 1879. I believe that the writer of the notation on the envelope meant to record the death of ANN Murin instead of Mary.

In Estate Record Book "F," Page 287, is the following entry: "ANN Murrin, Dec'd.-Greetings to Jacob H. Harmon – ANN Murrin died leaving no Will and The Court being satisfied as to your claim to the Administration you are ordered to 'manage & settle' (my words) her Estate and report back to this Court. Witnessed by A. J. Greer, Clerk. 6th Day of July 1879."

From this document, I would assume that A. J. Murrin had either remarried or Ann was a sister to A. J. Murrin and thus an Aunt of Marys. Robert J. Murrin had ten or eleven children according to Will Book I, and A. J. and an Ann Murrin were specifically mentioned in his Will, Robert J. Murrin being the father of A. J. and possibly the Ann whose estate Mary Murrin Harmon and husband were to settle.

In the January Term of Chancery Court in 1879, the final settlement of Ann Murrin's estate was recorded.

"Settlement of Ann Murrin Estate" . . . "leaving the sum of $8.50 in Admrs. Hands which sums to be paid to Mary Harmon, wife of the Admr. She having filed receipts from the other heirs for their respective shares of interest in said Estate."

It would appear from the reference above that this Mary Murrin Harmon was the descendant of A. J. and Charlotte Keeble Murrin.

JANE HENRY KEEBLE
1/12/1821 –

JANE HENRY KEEBLE

Jane Henry Keeble was born January 12, 1821, the daughter of Revolutionary War Veteran William Keeble and his wife, Mary Keeble Keeble. Jane was the youngest of eleven children born to this family.

It would appear that her childhood was beset with many problems. Her father, in his application for a pension in 1829, stated that the mother, Mary, "is sickly and unable to assist in making support for the family." This statement would suggest that the older children in the family had the care of the younger offspring, as well as preparing meals, household chores, and tending the garden so as to put food on the table.

In the application, William declared that Jane was "about four years of age." We know from the birthdate in the family Bible that Jane was double the age her father stated – she was eight years old at that time. He also avowed that Charlotte, her next older sister, was "aged about five years." Charlotte at that time was one month less than ten years of age. Were the two sisters of a diminutive size as to make one think they were younger than they really were? One has to leave that decision up to the reader's imagination.

I am sure that the applicant for a pension, in many cases, made dire explanations of their situation in order to receive compensation, but there had to be a modicum of truth in what he declared, for a government agent usually followed upon the particulars of the claim and would deny any claim falsely attested to.

Jane was thirteen years old when her father died. She was to inherit from his estate a bed containing 25 pounds of good feathers and other furniture for said bed. When Jane's mother died, her Will appeared to compensate Jane for staying at home and caring for her in her old age. Jane is the first of the children mentioned, and she left "my mare named Rache, my large red bedstead with all the furniture pertaining to the bed, five calico quilts and one white counter pin and a small chest." Mary died in 1855.

In the 1860 Census for Blount County, Tennessee, Jane was named first of the household occupants. She was listed as a Tenant. Apparently the property had not yet been divided. Living with her were Stephen Davis, Polly Banks Keeble Davis (Jane's sister), and the eight Davis children.

After the homeplace was disposed of, Jane stayed a month or two at each of her brother and sister's homes locally.

The oldest members of the Keeble families that I met in the early days of my search stated to me that as children they hated to see Jane coming to stay at their homes. They stated that she was a crotchety old woman who would do nothing to help her hosts and continually criticized the children whatever they were doing. The children in turn taunted her when they could get away with it. They composed a rhyme about her and sang it from memory to me in their old age.

Did she blame her brothers and sisters for being left at home with the care of her mother or was she just eccentric like her brothers, Thomas and Samuel? One would wonder what happened to the two beds and furniture she inherited. Did brothers and sisters have to cart those items from home to home when she changed residences? At the time of the 1870 Census, Jane was living with her sister, Rebecca Farmer, and family. In 1880 she was living adjacent to the home of James C. Dunlap, her sister Hannah's oldest son. We do not know her death date or where she is buried.

APPENDIX

(the lives and happenings of a few of the Keebles found while researching their ancestor's history)

LANSON W. KEEBLE (CABLE)

Never in any of the Keeble family records have I "come across" the given name LANSON. It is true that Mrs. Edith B. Little, in transcribing the marriages of Blount County in her first editions, listed a marriage between Lanson W. Keeble and Elizabeth A. Chambers with a marriage date of April 18, 1850. Indeed Edgar "Si" Keeble inquired repeatedly as to who Lanson W. Keeble was. He was one of the oldest living Keebles, and he could find nothing on the person or anyone who had ever known the individual. Other than Mrs. Little's book of Blount County Marriages, there was no other proof that such a person had inhabited Blount County.

In searching in the Blount County Courthouse and in the DEED Books of the County while investigating an entirely different matter, I discovered the origin of the name Lanson W. Keeble. One of the early scribes was not an able penman. His writing of the name LAWSON made the W look like an N. That error in writing gave us the name LANSON. Equally telling in the scribe's penmanship (spelling) was his use of a K instead of a C in Lawson W. Cable's last name. The scribe then used an "open A" following the K, which made the A look like a double E. Thus what appeared on the marriage license as Lanson W. Keeble to Mrs. Little was in fact the marriage of Lawson W. Cable and Elizabeth A. Chambers.

Mrs. Little, who had Cades Cove ancestors, removed the Lanson W. Keeble marriage from her subsequent editions of her book. Lawson W. Cable was a member of the Cable family, well known for the Cades Cove Cable Mill, which is still in existence.

For references, should you have doubts as to the authenticity of this information, I suggest you refer to the following Deed Books (DB) in the Register of Deeds Office in the Blount County Courthouse, Maryville, Tennessee.

Deed Book BB, Page 345, "D. B. Lawson vs: Lawson W. Kable et al,"
   March 4, 1867
Deed Book BB, Page 582.3, Lawson W. Cable
Deed Book Z, Page 535

JOHN KEEBLE

It would not be prudent to complete this volume without any mention of John Keeble. We know that William Keeble, Revolutionary War Veteran, had four children by a first mate, as stated in his Will. If he listed the children in their birth order, John was the oldest of the four. Did William bring his eldest son with him when he came to Tennessee in the spring of 1800 or is it possible that John Keeble came to Tennessee at a later date. We have not a clue.

John Keeble was in Blount County at an early date for according to Blount County records, John Keeble married Catherine Ledbetter on September 3, 1819. We do not know John's birthdate, as none of the records pertaining to him give his natal date. For John to have been William's son in his first family, he would have had to been born prior to 1800, as the father married in 1799. If this John was born in the 1790s, his age would have been within reason for marriage at that time.

John's bride was the widow of Lewis Ledbetter. Catherine is mentioned in Lewis Ledbetter's estate, which was filed in Blount County. According to records, Catherine was born about 1790 and died in the spring of 1870. Information about John's life has been difficult to obtain and what documents exist are indefinite to a great degree.

Photostats from the National Archives list John Kibble, Private, in Capt. Edward Buchanan's Company in the War of 1812. He is listed in the Muster Roll of a Company of East Tennessee drafted Militia under the command of Capt. Buchanan in the Regiment commanded by Colonel Samuel Wear in the service of the United States from the 10th of January to the 20th of May in 1814.

Of the few records of John and Catherine (Ledbetter) Keeble that I have found are the following:

On the 1st day of October personally appeared William Walker, a Justice of the Peace for McMinn County, who being duly sworn states that he is William H. Walker and was present and saw John Kibble and Catherine Kibble married (date left blank) and the John Kibble died the 27th of December 1846 and that Catherine has remained a widow.

The cover Sheet had the following information.
99791 Feb. 26, 1852
C. Kibble, wid.   Third Aud.' Office
Jno. Kibble, Dec'd.   13 May 1852
Catherine Kibble widow of John Kibble
War of 1812 from <u>Blount County, Tennessee</u>

On November 29, 1850 Catherine Kibble appeared before William Rogers, Justice of the Peace, McMinn County, Tennessee, to make application for Bounty Land due Veterans of the War of 1812.

She states that she is aged about fifty six years and the Widow of John Kibble, who was a Private soldier in the Tennessee Militia in the Creek War of 1813-that he was drafted at Blount County, Tennessee for the term of six months and served in said War for six months and served out the time for which he was drafted. She does not remember the date of their marriage but that John Kibble died on the 27th day of December 1846 and that she has remained a widow. She makes Declaration for the purpose of obtaining bounty land to which she may be entitled under the Law of Congress granting Bounty Land to those who may have been engaged in the military service of The United States, passed the 28th day of September 1850, and she wishes her Warrant to be sent to her Agent, James Hickey, Calhoun, Tennessee.   Her
                                Catherine (X) Kibble
                                       Mark

I should state that in Catherine's application for Bounty Land, important blanks were left unanswered, such as where born, personal features (color of hair, eyes and complexion), and birth date. To have completed these blanks for John Kibble would have aided us immeasurably in determining whether this John was the son of "our" William Keeble.

<u>Children of John Kibble and Catherine Ledbetter Kibble</u>

Elias Kibble – A Cherokee War Veteran	Married Martha C. Jones
William A. Kibble – Mexican War Pensioner	Married Lucinda Coxey
James Kibble	Married Mary Reed
George W. Kibble	An Invalid*
Lidia Kibble	An Invalid*
Ruth Kibble	Married Isaac Cannon

*Helpless and had to be cared for by the family.

WAR RECORD OF ELIAS KIBBLE, ELDEST SON OF JOHN KIBBLE

<u>May 25, 1854</u> – Kibble, aged 40 years, a resident of McMinn County, Tennessee, states he was a Volunteer for service on July 10, 1837, as a private soldier in a company of Mountain Volunteers commanded by Capt. James Morrow in a Regiment commanded by Col. Powell in the removal of the Cherokee Indians. He volunteered at Ft. Cass. Tenn. He never received a discharge (written) and was dismissed, as was the rest of the company, on July 10, 1838, at Ft. Cass, Tenn.

APPLICATION FOR BOUNTY LAND

Calhoun, Tennessee, <u>May 29, 1854</u> – One John Hambright sends above to Washington. Sirs: Please find claim of Elias Kibble for Bounty Land. Mr. Kibble is an illiterate man and does not know how his name is spelled on the Roll of Capt. Morrow. William Varnell was present when he made his declaration and who served in the same company as Mr. Kibble. He thinks the name is spelled Cibble.

<u>March 8, 1880</u> – State of Tennessee, County of Decatur – Kibble appeared before John McMillan, Clerk of County Court, Decatur, Co., stated he was about 64 years of age, and served as a private commanded by Capt. Morris, 1st East Tenn. Regiment, in War of 1836. For two years prior to his enlistment, he was a farmer living in McMinn County, Tennessee. He lived in Ray (Rhea) County at the commencement of Late War (Civil). He lay out in the mountains to keep from being conscripted for about two years during the late war and was maltreated and abused by the confederate soldiers on the account of his loyalty. Had the last horse taken from him by the confederate soldiers on account of his loyalty and the last bushel of corn for contending for the Union.

He states he was wounded near Conasagu in what was then called the Cherokee Nation, now East Tennessee, in the line of duty on a march from Ella Town, Georgia, to Ft. Maria, was suddenly dashed from his horse and struck a snag which passed through the left thigh which caused a very bad wound lacerating the muscles and a large artery of the left thigh which had since terminated in what the doctors call aneurism of the artery – was carried from the said place to Mr. Ross's was treated by the Sgt. Of the Command – that he has never had any violent disease of acute character since but at times has intermittent fever. He has not been able to perform manual labor since the wound was inflicted. Was the owner of 300 Acres at time he was wounded (1837) but had to sell said land for support and is destitute of resources.

It has been 45 years and a four year siege of war so that the officers and soldiers he knew in the Cherokee War are dead or removed from the area.

October 14, 1880: State of different places Elias Kibble has lived since he received his wound: In 1838 he lived in McMinn County, Tenn. Lived there about four years and went to Linkin Co., Georgia, lived there three years and moved to Cole County, Missouri near Jefferson City and lived there three years. Then to Arkansas near Little Rock for six years, from there to the City of Memphis, Tenn. I lived there three years and then moved back to East. Tenn. And McMinn County where he lived four years, then to Ray County stayed there an undetermined number of years and then returned to McMinn County. In the "Late War" (Civil War) he had to lay out in the mountains of East. Tenn. To keep from being conscripted. Lived since the late war in "Marriaso Co. Tenn. And Franklin Co. Alabama from there to Decatur, Co., Tenn. Where I now am living. I have little recollections of the Post Offices of my address at each place.
****

Feb. 16, 1881 – War Department – Adjutant General's Office – Washington, D.C., Cherokee War

Respectfully returned to the Commissioner of Pensions: This report says that Elias Kibble, Private, was as stated above, from July 1837 to Apr. 30, 1838. No evidence of disability of any nature during his term of service.
****

March 8, 1881 – Elias Kibble again makes a statement: State of Tennessee, Decatur, Co.

Statement much the same as the above statement. Additional information: He now says that his injury in the war has been "praying on me ever since inflicted," which has caused total disability. He knows of no one who acted as a commissioned officer in the war who is available for a statement. "Daniel Ford was an Orderly of my company, was 2nd. Sargent in said Co. about the time I received my wound." He has written four letters to Ray County attempting to get someone to attest to his loyalty during the Late War, as he was living in Ray County at the time. He has received no replies other than that those addressed had moved to parts unknown. He

states he has a wife and four small children who are dependent on him for support. He hopes for an early settlement of his claim.
****

November 14, 1881 – Elias Kibble again appears before John McMillan, Clerk of County of Decatur, Tenn. In it he gives a more graphic picture of his receiving his injury. "That on a march in the Summer of 1836 while on a march from New Town, Ga. To Duck Town, Tenn. In the company commanded at that time by Capt. Marro he was suddenly thrown from his horse by the horse being frightened and fell on a snag which passed through the left thigh just above the knee on the left side inflicting a very serious wound lacerating some of the large Blood Vessels of the thigh causing what Physicians call anurism inlarged arteries so as to inable me from walking without a great deal of pain and lameness. Orr was 1st Orderly but died about the time I was wounded. Then Daniel Ford took his place at the time the said wound occurred and assisted in getting me carried to a dwelling house. Mr. Ross's in what is now called Bradley County, Tenn. Where I remained for several months until the Command in which I was a member was taken up winter quarters in the same county. Then I was carried back to the Command of Ft. Morrow there remained in the Hospital and was treated by the Reg't Surgeon for about four months or until I was mustered out of said service."

Deponent further states that Surgeon Crain stated at several times that he would be always cripple on account of said wound. "I ask that my said Insurance Claim be reconsidered and that a Minute Examination be made upon the old records in regard to my said claim. Knowing that thousands of invalids are now realizing the benefits of Ind. Pensions from slight disabilities in the late war that never was in any actual service, while I am yet groping my way through from year 1836 to the present time suffering the pains and afflictions of a wound that has set up a lifetime disability and have realized nothing and am of destitute circumstances of infirm age and physical debility."
****

May 24, 1882 – State of Tennessee, Hardin County: H. R. Hinkle, County Court Clerk writes: "Elias Kibble appears before him to state: I lived in McMinn County, Tenn. From my infancy until 1841. I then removed to Lumpkins Co. Ga. Where I lived until 1844. Then back to McMinn County, where I remained until 1847. I then went to New Madrid County, Missouri and remained two years – then I went to Memphis, Tenn. Where I remained two years. I then returned to East Tenn. Where I remained until after the war of rebellion. I then lived in Warren County, Tenn. Until 1867. Since which time I have lived in Decatur Co. and Hardin Co. Tenn. " He then describes his injury and how obtained and that it made him a permanent cripple. Otherwise his health has been reasonably good and he has not had any regular physician since that time. He has tried to follow the occupation of farming since his discharge from the Army, when able to do anything, but has not been able to do a "half-a-mans work." "Dr's. Johnson & McWhirter both of East Tenn. furnished him linament at diff. Times to go on my leg after I left the army. They, I think, are both dead. My disability gradually increases as I grow older."

Monday, 5th of July 1852: <u>THE STATE OF TENNESSEE vs WILLIAM KEEBLE</u>

"In this case a Warrant and other papers having been returned to Court accusing the said defendant of being father of a Bastard Child of which one Elizabeth Boling was delivered on the 5th of December, 1851, but because it does not appear from said papers and proceedings had before the Justice that said child was born in Blount County:

It is therefore ordered by the Court that the said proceedings be quashed and that the defendant go hence and that the clerk tax and certify that the legal costs for the inspection of this Court . . ."

The subject of this court case is William McCutchin Keeble.

Elizabeth Boling then took her suit to a Sevier county, Tennessee, for trial and the Court there stated that the act didn't happen in Sevier County and therefore again dismissed the proceedings in that county.

Mary (Polly) Keeble Helton told me that when her father and mother married August 14, 1862, and went into housekeeping, this child, Sally Boling, was left on their doorstep. I had assumed that the child was a foundling. In the record above, it is evident that the child was eleven years of age in 1862. Polly quoted her mother as saying that she was the only woman she knew who started out married life with a half raised daughter.

Sally was raised in the household as a sister to Polly and her brothers and sisters; however, the 1860 Census lists her as Sally Bolen in the Keeble household.

The interesting thing to me was the way in which I learned about this "Case."

The first time I went to See Aunt Polly Helton, I asked for information about Polly's mother, father, and siblings. She gave me all the information I requested. Her mind was sharp and she had the names and dates of all her brothers and sisters. I thought I had the complete line.

On my second visit to see Aunt Polly, her first remark was, "You didn't ask me about Sally." I had heard nothing of a Sally Keeble and so stated to her. She then stated that Sally had been left on her parents' doorstep after they were married. At that time, I knew nothing of the lawsuits in Blount and Sevier Counties by the mother of the child seeking remuneration from the apparent father, William McCutchin Keeble. One wonders if Aunt Polly had the real truth of the situation.

According to the lawsuit, Sally was born December 5, 1851, to Elizabeth Boling, and the two courts in which the case was tried were unable to determine if the child was conceived in Blount or Sevier County and thus dismissed the suits. Aunt Polly's parents were married in 1862.

The 1860 Census for Sevier County, Tennessee, lists Sally in the William Keeble household as Sally Bolen. She would have been nine years of age at that time and seven years of age when Polly's parents were married in 1862. I had assumed from Aunt Polly's explanation that Sally was a foundling left on her father's doorstep.

William McCutchin Keeble's house sat on the Blount-Sevier County line.

UNNAMED KEEBLE GOES TO TEXAS

According to Blount County Records, in December of 1817, "William Keeble, an orphan boy, now of the age of seven years is bound to William Keeble, Sr. until he arrives at the age of twenty-one years." We have no idea who this child belonged to or from whence he came to live with William and Mary Keeble. The court record just does not reveal that information.

It is my suspicion that this William Keeble was probably the unnamed Keeble who purchased a yoke of oxen from Martin McTeer of the Ellejoy Community of Blount County, as he was desiring to go to Texas. The time of the sale was apparently sometime in the 1850-1860s.

Carl McTeer, Great Grandson of Martin McTeer, took me to the scene where the oxen had pastured prior to being sold to Keeble. He told me the story repeated often by his father, A. J. McTeer, who was told the story by his father, Jim. It seems Keeble wanted to join the trek of Tennesseans west to Texas, and he approached Martin McTeer to ascertain if McTeer would sell his high stepping short-horn Durham cattle that were lean and tough and which stepped out like horses. The ordinary oxen were a slow moving lot. Certainly wagons pulled by oxen were the common means of travel to the west.

It is said that the usual price for a pair of oxen at that time was about $50.00. McTeer would not consider parting with these animals for that price and Keeble left. Keeble returned later and offered McTeer $125.00 for the pair of steers, and Mr. McTeer could not refuse that price and gave the purchaser the yoke also in the deal. Keeble then asked for the big bell that one of the oxen had around his neck. He explained that he wouldn't have much grain to feed them, and the bell would help him find them as they foraged on the range when he turned them out to pasture in Texas. McTeer told him to take the bell, which was valuable in itself at that time. Farmers of that era knew the sound of their own cowbells, and many times the particular sound of their neighbors' cattle bells.

Keeble soon left for Texas, the story says, to the Amarillo area about 1200 miles from the McTeer farm. It is said Keeble entered a tract of land there and turned the animals out to graze. For some time, the steers came to the house each night for a little bit of grain their master could give them, then the animals returned to the house more infrequently, perhaps a couple times a week and then not at all.

Keeble mounted his horse and rode over his land and could not find the cattle. He started heading eastward over the trail he had used in going to Texas. Every few miles he would find someone who had seen the tired, gaunt, long-legged animals traveling east alone. When Keeble reached the Mississippi River to the bank opposite Memphis (there was no bridge at that time, only a ferry), the ferryman remembered encountering the animals. The cattle had arrived several days before and had tried to walk onto the ferry. The operator stopped them, thinking the owner would soon arrive to get them.

Each day the animals tried to enter the ferry and were denied admittance, and he drove them away. The boatman was puzzled by the tired, hungry animals remaining there. Then one morning the animals were gone. There were tracks in the mud near the ferry at the river's bank, which showed that the animals had entered the water. That was the story that the boat operator told Keeble. Their master, in disbelief, returned to Texas, never believing that the oxen could have navigated the mile wide river and its swift current.

A few weeks later in the Ellejoy Community of Blount County, A. J. McTeer went to awaken his father, Jim, and told him that he heard the bell of Martin's oxen and his exact words were: "Martin's steers are back. I hear their bell up there in the old pasture. 'Couldn't be' replied the father, 'they're in Texas.'" But, he too heard the bell and knowing the bell's sound had to investigate for himself. In the morning, father and son went to the old pasture and found the gaunt, long-legged mud-caked animals. One of the animals licked Jim's arm.

Jim and A. J. went immediately to tell Martin about the return of the steers. Martin wrote to Keeble and from the correspondence which followed was able to confirm the trail of the homesick animals from Texas.

Martin McTeer's last letter to Keeble contained a bank draft for $125.00 and a letter which said, "Here's your money back. If those steers love me that much, you needn't come back for them."

I have written to Amarillo, Texas, in an attempt to locate the Keeble family tree to no avail. The above article was published in the <u>Amarillo Daily Newspaper</u>.

Surprise of surprises, a young man, Donald Appling, who had been one of my students when I taught school in Townsend, Blount County, Tennessee, in the 1950s wrote to state that he had checked the courthouse in Amarillo attempting to assist me, but he could find no record of the Keeble name there. Thus I was never able to determine the given name of the purchaser of McTeer's long-legged oxen. There is the distant possibility that this William Keeble is the son of William and his slave Sarah. As with our suggestion that William brought his slave with him when he came to Tennessee, the younger generation of the family knew nothing of the origin of either John or William, who were both in Blount County at an early date. The only other possibility is that this William was the child sent to William Keeble of Blount County to raise in 1817. We have not a clue as to whose child he was or from whence he came, Virginia or Maryland.

A CIVIL WAR EXPERIENCE OF JAMES T. (THOMAS) KEEBLE

James T. Keeble was born July 2, 1847, the first child of William McCutchin Keeble and his first wife, Mary Townsend. He enlisted in the Third Tennessee Volunteer Cavalry in Company "H" on September 28, 1863, and was mustered into service on November 12, 1863. He reported that he was eighteen years of age at the time of enlistment but in truth he was just two months over sixteen.

While in service, he was captured by the southern forces. He was stripped of his horse and uniform and was forced to put on a Confederate uniform. He was being taken to the base Confederate camp and told to ride on the back of a horse behind one of the enemy soldiers.

Keeble knew the terrain they would pass through and contemplated how he might escape. It was a dark night and difficult to see as they wended their way. The horses and their riders were filing single file along the edge of a steep bank as the path or road led. At a certain spot, Keeble fell off the horse and rolled down the embankment and lay very still. The Rebels emptied their pistols and rifles down into the vegetation; miraculously James was not hit.

The Confederates remarked that they were sure he was dead, for if he had survived, they would have heard him moan, and so they continued on without him. After they were out of hearing, he went up across the road to the top of the hill, stopping only long enough to cut himself a walking stick from a sapling along the way. Looking around as best he could at the hilltop, he saw a large hollow log. He probed the interior of the log and the walking stick and found the log vacant. He was forced to enter the log from the end, feet first, and soon fell asleep with his head completely inside the log.

After sleeping what he considered a long time, he was awakened by a scratching on the log and screams of a panther. The moon was shining by this time, and he could see something dark sticking its head in the hole near his head. Keeble got his walking stick into position and when the panther stuck his head in the hole the second time, James struck the panther between the eyes with a sharp jab. The panther left screaming and did not return.

When daylight came, Keeble eased out of the log, looked around, and saw an open field off in the distance and a small slave house. He went to the house, and a black slave woman met him at the door. He told her his experience of the night before and she told him, "The southerners were camping close by just out of sight, and that they will be coming and going by all day; but I can put you under the floor where I have some chickens. I will give you a tin cup and when you hear me tell someone I'm going to water my chickens, you hold the cup up next to the crack and I will give you some water."

She raised the planks and Keeble descended into the crawl space with the tin cup. This was his hiding place for three days. Each day a hen came under the floor and laid an egg. Keeble broke the shell and swallowed the egg, and this was his only ration for those days.

During this time, a battle raged in the area, and finally the Rebels were driven off. James came from under the cabin, and the black woman directed him as to which direction she thought he ought to go to get back to his forces. He was so weak and stiff he could hardly walk but still had his walking stick for support.

When he reached camp dressed in the gray uniform, his buddies did not recognize him, and he took a lot of derision, cat calls, and laughter about giving his side hell last night, etc. When he got close enough for them to recognize him, they hollered, "Oh yes, I would come creeping in" and then when they saw his condition and realized he had been captured, they ran to meet him and carried him into camp and put him to bed. Keeble was in Atlanta with Sherman and was in the army that marched to the sea and up through the coastal cities.

James married Prudence Caroline Jenkins, daughter of Laban Jenkins and Eliz. Lewellyn in 1868 and fathered six girls, namely Laban Elizabeth, Mary Ann, Sally, Marinda, Nancy, and Eliza. He died in November of 1880.

The William McCutchin Keeble families were raised in Sevier and Blount Counties, Tennessee. The family relationships of the Keebles in this instance is one that gives genealogist's trouble.

I was told that this man was a half brother of Laban Keeble, my wife's grandfather. As I told earlier, James was the first child born to William

174

McCutchin Keeble and Mary Townsend Keeble. They were married in 1845 and had four other children.

Laban Keeble was the eighth child of nine children born to William McCutchin Keeble and his second wife, Nancy Jenkins Keeble, who married in 1862, Laban being born December 10, 1879. Thus, there is a time lapse of 32 years between the birth of these two half-brothers.

The Civil War story was related to me by Mrs. Ella Floyd Tarwater in the year 1950 and was written just as she related it.

MARION KEEBLE

Marion Keeble was born July 9, 1840, the second child and only son of Richard Porter Keeble and his wife, Elizabeth Rhea Keeble. He and his sister, Margaret, were raised in Walland, Tennessee, at the site of their father's cabin beside Little River.

As has been stated in his father's biography, Marion went to Virginia in 1857. This was the same year that his uncle Thomas Keeble, as Executor of his father's estate, deemed it necessary to travel to Virginia to ascertain what inheritance the children of William Keeble, Revolutionary War Veteran, were to expect as a result of his father's statement in his Will that there would be an inheritance from both his father and mother's side of the family. It would seem logical that some other member of the immediate family would accompany Thomas and report back to the family what could be expected in inheritance.

Marion, however, did not return home with Thomas. Were there still family ties close enough for a seventeen year old to live and find employment there? It has always been my assumption that Thomas and Marion went to Fauquier County, Virginia, to search for the estates of Thomas's grandparents since William and Mary came from there to Blount County.

I was surprised to find that in the 1860 Census from Chesterfield County, Virginia, Marion Keeble, age 20, a male farmer born in Tennessee, was living in the home of Philip P. Johnson, age 46, a male farmer born in Virginia and having real estate worth $41,000. The value of Mr. Johnson's personal estate was $8,600.00. Also living in the house was Edward A. Johnson, age 44, a male, Major 6th Reg. USA. The value of his personal estate was $4,000. Edward was also born in Virginia.

I know of no family connection with the Johnson name or how Marion gravitated to Chesterfield County. The Census Report details that this particular schedule was of the inhabitants in the Northern District of Chesterfield County and the Post Office address was Manchester.

Richard Keeble, in his Declaration for Redress as a result of Federal troops taking his crops in Blount County stated that he had not heard from his son for several years, and when he heard that Marion had entered the Army of the Confederacy, he had a letter written to his son advising him that he was on the "wrong side" and to come home.

Through records obtained by Mrs. Bobbie G. Young, a descendant of Marion, on a recent visit to Washington, D.C. and a search in the National Archives, we have a detailed account of Marion's military record.

For a quick review of history and the rapidity of Marion's enlistment, these facts are given.

April 13, 1861 – Fort Sumter surrender to General Beauregard.

April 14, 1861 – President Lincoln issued his proclamation declaring the Gulf States in rebellion.

April 17, 1861 – An Ordinance of Secession passed the Virginia Convention and the Commonwealth cast her fortune with the Southern Confederacy.

April 20, 1861 – Robert E. Lee resigned his commission as Colonel in the U.S. Army. Lee went from Washington to Richmond and was honored by a formal presentation to the convention. The governor appointed him Major General of the military forces of Virginia. The appointment was confirmed more by acclamation than by a formal vote on April 23rd.

There was universal public rejoicing in Richmond over the appointment and immediately the men of the city and surrounding area rushed to volunteer for the cause. Church bells pealed and the entire population was caught up in a patriotic frenzy.

On the same day that Lee accepted the leadership of the Virginia military forces on April 23rd, Marion Keeble enrolled for active service. He enrolled in Manchester, as he was living there. What part Major Edward Johnson played in Marion's enlistment we can only surmise. Did the Major resign his commission as Lee had done? Certainly Marion was in a position in the Johnson household to know the momentous events taking place in close proximity to his residence.

Manchester lay on the southwest bank of the James River, immediately across from Richmond. There were three bridges connecting Manchester with Richmond, Mayo's Bridge for passenger traffic and two railroad bridges, the Richmond and Louisville, and the Richmond and Petersburg railroads.

After enrolling in the Confederacy in the presence of Captain William B. Ball, Marion crossed the river over into Richmond that same day and was mustered into service by Lt. Col. Seldon. He had with him his horse which he valued at $100.00 and equipment worth $10.00. He appeared on the company muster roll April 23rd to June 30th 1861, having been assigned to Company B, 4th Regiment of the Virginia Cavalry as a Private.

If you have read any of the narration's of that point in history in the Richmond area, men and boys start arriving from all other Virginia. They came in such numbers that there was no place to house them. Citizens opened their homes and took the "boys" in and fed them from their tables, then volunteers started coming from other states with the same persuasion, adding to the confusion. This led to the need for immediate organization. Marion had enlisted early so does not appear to have been involved in this pressure of enlistment.

According to his papers, he was nineteen years of age when he enrolled. He was first assigned to Company B, which was called the Chesterfield Cavalry. One would assume that it was made up primarily of men from Chesterfield County.

Now comes the evidence of the large number of volunteers: Company B soon became Company B, 4th Regiment Virginia Cavalry. This regiment was formed September 19, 1861, of six unattached companies in Virginia Cavalry. These men had enlisted for 12 months. Soon three other unattached companies were added to the organization, and it was again reorganized on May 23, 1862. Under the new organization, the men enlisted for the "duration." The leader of the Virginia Cavalry was J. E. B. (Jeb) Stuart.

On October 31, 1861, Marion's muster roll was taken at a camp near Leesburg, Virginia. According to that report, he had traveled 14 miles to a rendezvous. Subsequent papers show that he was present for muster roll call January and February 1862.

There was no further notation on our subject until June 9, 1863, when the record states that he was captured at Stephensburg, Virginia. He continued to be listed on the company muster roll for April 30 – July 30, 1863, with the notation of his capture at Stephensburg June 9, 1863.

The scribe for the company made an error in his spelling of the town of capture. The village was Stevensburg and was approximately four miles south of Brandy Station on the railroad and six miles southeast of Culpepper. Culpepper is just south of the Rappahannock River, this river being the northern boundary of Virginia.

At this point I would like to give some background on the leader of the Virginia Cavalry.

"Jeb" Stuart, Beau Sabreur of the south, was a dashing character. On more than one occasion, he had led his Cavalry around McClellan's whole army. With a cavalry force of approximately 1200, moving with great speed and secrecy, he had ridden around the Union's right far to the rear and had returned by the left flank. Military critics considered the act "rash," but he thrilled the south with this spectacular stunt. In doing this act, he was able to bring to General Lee information about the size of McClellan's troops and where the troops were placed.

Records relay the facts that Jeb and his cavalry covered eighty miles in 27 hours, with a loss of one wounded and two missing. Lee regarded Stuart as "the eyes of the Army." There was criticism that Stuart was too bold in his maneuvers and put his men in harms way. He was a picturesque soldier and a real showman. His uniform was colorful, a gray cloak lined with red. He often wore a red flower in his jacket lapel. His hat was cocked to one side, with a gilt start that held a peacock plume. He always rode a spirited steed. He liked his troops to be in a happy frame of mind but prohibited drinking, swearing, and licentiousness. He was idolized by the younger men of the cavalry. General Lee appeared to regard him almost as a son. Lee thought of him as an ideal soldier.

Certainly Marion, being a young man, was caught up in this spirited adventure. Marion was in a group led by Lt. Goldsborough on June 9th near Culpepper, Virginia. The Lt. had been ordered by Stuart to take his forces to a Colonel Butler near Stevensburg to learn if Butler knew anything of the enemy's preparations in that area. Goldsborough was a fine, handsome young officer, but he had just joined the staff a few days prior and was inexperienced. He was not cautious as a staff officer, and he rode up to a body of troops thinking they were Confederates, when actually they were Union Troops. It is explained that there was so much dust on the men's uniforms that it was difficult to tell the blue from the gray. Thus, Goldsborough and his troops were taken prisoner, including Marion.

A document in Marion's papers is an invoice from the Confederate States to Marion Keeble dated June 9, 1863, the date of his capture, stating "to the value of horse killed in an engagement with the enemy at Stephensburg, Virginia, June 9, 1863, and valued at $300.00." Marion certified on his honor that the horse above referred to was killed in an engagement with the enemy and valued as stated above on the muster roll of the company. Whether this invoice was filled out prior to his capture is not clear. On August 10, 1863, Marion received from the Quartermaster C. S. Army $300,00 in payment of the account.

Marion had been in the midst of a colorful but deadly arena. He next appears on the Roll of Prisoners of War, paroled June 11, 1863, until exchanged at headquarters Army of the Potomac and forwarded to Washington, D.C. on June 12, 1863, to be confined in Old Capitol Prison, from which he is paroled on June 25, 1863.

According to records in the fine, when Marion was taken prisoner, he was one of the 858 soldiers held. These men were paroled for exchange from Washington and taken by boat to City Point, Virginia. This place was on the James River near its juncture with the Appomattox River. The Federal Army had captured this neck of land at the mouth of the James River and the Confederate Army had formed a line immediately to the north to keep the Federal forces from going up the James River to Richmond and capturing it from the rear.

A recorded document in the file relates "received, City Point, Virginia, June 30, 1863, from Major John E. Mulford, 8th Infantry, New York Volunteers eight hundred fifty eight (858) Confederate Prisoners of War paroled for exchange. One officer, One Surgeon, One Chaplain and four citizens."

On June 30th Marion is listed on the Receipt Roll for an issue of clothing. On July 10th after exchange, he got a clothing allowance for three quarters of 1863. I do not know how he would have gotten a clothing allowance on June 30th unless he was exchanged prior to the papers having been filled out.

From this point we see a different soldier. He had been restored to his old company, but his heart apparently was no longer in the fight. It may have been that seeing the carnage wrought in the Battle of Stevensburg and having his horse shot out from under him or the death of his buddies around him may have weakened his resolve. The mostly likely reason for his change in attitudes was caused by Lt. Goldsborough, as his leader, leading Marion's Company headlong into battle thinking they were joining other troops on the Confederate side, when in fact he led them into a trap with the Federals precipitated by his inexperience. This error in judgment had caused 858 men to be captured and untold numbers to be killed along with their gallant steeds.

Following this harrowing experience, Marion was forced to endure prison encampments and prisons where he probably contracted a disease that remained with him throughout the remaining years of his life.

On October 14, 1863, Marion Keeble appears on a register of Receiving and Wayside Hospital or General Hospital #9, Richmond, Virginia. Apparently they didn't have room or were not treating his kind of illness, for the same day he was transferred to the register of Chimborazo Hospital #2, Richmond, with a condition which appears to be "Intrex Fever." He remained at this hospital, and October 23rd there is a notation on his record, "see personal papers of Louis B. Madison, Chaplain."

The next notation he appears on the Muster Roll for the company for September 30 – October 31 with a notation "absent-sick." He was dismissed from the hospital and returned to duty on December 8.
On December 17, he was admitted to C. S. A. General Hospital in Charlottesville, Virginia, with a "Hepatic Disorder." This apparently is a liver malady with jaundice being a common result. He was then transferred to Richmond on January 23, 1864 where he was again received at the

Receiving and Wayside Hospital or General Hospital #9 on January 24. On February 5, 1864, he was again admitted to Chimborazo Hospital #2 in Richmond with the notation "Pneumonia." He was furloughed on April 7th for thirty days by the company commander.

Marion next appears on the Register of the Medical Director's Office, Richmond, under the topic Furloughs and Leaves of Absence. Orders received February 23 for an Order dated February 20 from Chimborazo Hospital with a notation from Major Pegram.

On the Muster Roll dated November 5, 1864, but recorded for March and April 1864, it states that Marion was last paid January 1, 1864. At the November 5th recording, the notation on the card was "absent" and then under it "absent without leave."

Since Marion had been living with the Johnsons near Manchester just across the river from Richmond prior to the war, one would surmise that he spent his 30 days' furlough at the plantation and anytime after that when well enough, he would repair to those familiar surroundings.

It was probably to the Johnson home that Richard Keeble, the father, mailed his son the letter which advised Marion that he was on the "wrong side" and to "come home." I would assume that the father knew nothing of his son's cavalry record nor the fact that he rode with Jeb Stuart and indeed had paraded before and seen Robert E. Lee in person. He had been in the thick of many a battle, had ridden on numerous charges and scouting parties. He had helped protect the flanks of the armies as they marched through the campaigns. That his life had been spared was a miracle in itself; now his father tells him to come home, that he is on the wrong side. How depressing when you have given your entire self to a cause and sickness of body and spirit have overtaken you!

Marion came home to Tennessee a sick man. Once here he decided to stay, for on December 21, 1864, he married in Blount County Martha Jane Clark, daughter of John Clark and Matilda Thompson Clark. From this marriage, 13 children were born:

Nancy Ann Keeble	B: 9/23/1865	D: 9/23/1865
Elizabeth Jane Keeble	B: 9/19/1866	M: Robert M. Farmer 5/29/1890
Richard Porter Keeble	B: 8/06/1868	M: Ora Trotter 10/ /1910
John Ellison Keeble	B: 8/11/1869	M: Catherine J. Headrick
Margaret Clementine Keeble	B: 3/08/1871	M: Samuel Jackson Gamble 6/15/1890
Edward George Keeble	B: 4/04/1872	M: Mary Catherine Hatcher 9/09/1894
Matilda Clarinda Keeble	B: 6/01/1874	M: William Jack Hatcher 10/13/1894
Mary Louisa Keeble	B: 10/28/18	M: Joseph H. Farmer 7/18/1894
Marion Priscilla Keeble	B: 9/05/1878	M: Riley A. Graves 3/29/1895
Henry Fitzhugh Keeble	B: 10/28/1880	D: 12/3/1880
Martha Addline Keeble	B: 9/21/1882	M: Warren Stanford Perkins 7/04/1911
Sina Gertrude Keeble	B: 3/03/1887	M: James G. McFadden 3/12/1912
Rosa Lee Keeble	B: 5/30/1890	D: 5/30/1890

The mother, Martha Jane Clark Keeble, was born April 16, 1844.

The 1870 Census for Blount County, Tennessee, lists Marion as a farm laborer and wife, Martha Jane, as a housekeeper. The first three children were listed as living in the household.

Marion Keeble died May 5, 1890, when he was only fifty years of age. His wife died in the same year, leaving several minor children. Both of the deaths were ruled as caused by Cholera. Martha died December 22, 1890.

In discussing these deaths with a doctor friend, I learned the following: He stated that "intrax," as listed on Marion's record, was Intestinal Diarrhea or what we now commonly call Amoebic Dysentery. He said it was quite common with Civil War soldiers. It was an infectious inflammatory disease of the colon, resulting in severe pain and diarrhea. The "Hepatic Disorder," also mentioned in the records, would follow right along with the Inthrax Fever diagnosis. The doctor then stated, "It probably was Cholera." They had no way of killing the infection at that time – you endured it for the remainder of your life." Cholera had the same symptoms as Amoebic Dysentery but was caused by a different bacterium. This apparently then was the reason for the change in Marion as a solder and for his short life span. It was the opinion of the doctor that Martha probably became infected with the same disorder through long-time contact with her infected husband.

The death of the parents left seven children under the age of 21. They were entered in the Orphan's Book at the Blount County Courthouse and put under the care of their grandfather, Richard Keeble, with whom they lived until his death in 1894.

As each child became of age or married, they were given their share of their grandfather's estate and released from Court custody.

Both Martha Jane and Marion Keeble are buried in the Keeble Chapel Cemetery. Their graves are marked with headstones.

KEEBLE VS. KEEBLE
Chancery Court Suit – Blount County, Tennessee
Filed March 29, 1867

One might surmise that a suit headed as above would be a divorce case. However, this is a dispute of brother against brother. The proceedings are full of information of the Keeble family and problems of the time. It is important to the narrative to give some background information. Manly and Richard Keeble, sons of William Keeble, Revolutionary War Veteran, married sisters Rebecca and Elizabeth Rhea. The girls' father was Jesse Rhea, who departed this life in 1858 in Monroe County, Tennessee. Jesse was the father of fourteen children; and to each child or their heirs, he left $995.16, as well as an estate to his second wife, Amelia. He appointed his son, William Rhea, and Elisha E. Griffith, J.P., Executors. Son William refused to act as Executor, and E. E. Griffith took on the task alone.

In the settlement procedure during the Civil War, the shares of six of the children were confiscated by the Confederate Government.

Depositions in the file of the Jesse Rhea Estate filed in Monroe County relate this message: "E. E. Griffith answers that William Rhea refused to act as Exec. and that he, Griffith, settled the Estate and paid all the resident heirs their share that he had no way of communicating with or sending money to the heirs in the Northern States outside of Confederate States and had the funds for those non-residents in his hands until the Confederate Government brought suit against him and confiscated their shares, a sum of $5,970.96. Witnesses testify that during the early part of the War, the County was strongly Rebel and those with Union Sentiment were held in subjection; that in 1861 – 1862, some Union Men were mobbed in Madisonville; that Thomas J. Campbell, a Major in the Confederate Army, was in charge of confiscation of property of Union Men and was Judge Advocate when some Union Men were condemned of bridge burning; that all were afraid of not obeying his orders. Chancellor decrees that Griffith pay the six heirs their shares, 'even though confiscated.'" Griffith appeals to the Tennessee Supreme Court.

For the genealogists, of the six families who left the area, four went to Illinois: Mary Coulter, wife of John Coulter, Margaret Stephens, Eveline, wife of John Magill (or McGill), and Levina, wife of John Stephens. Son

Lewis Rhea went to Oregon and son Riley to California. Now to get on with our narrative about the Keeble brothers.

William Keeble, father of Manly and Richard, died in 1834. His wife, Mary, being much younger, lived until 1855. Each of the children shared in their father's estate, but Manly had apparently already borrowed against his share so that when the estate was settled, he had little or nothing coming to him.

Now, four years later, Rebecca Rhea Keeble was to inherit a portion of her father's estate. Rebecca took action promptly to protect her inheritance from her husband's wasteful ways. Rebecca went to Monroe County and with her brother William, as her next friend, petitioned the Court to exclude her husband from receiving any part of her inheritance. The seriousness of her charges are outlined in her declaration. "Your Oratrix further states and will show your Honor that the said Manly Keeble is wholly insolvent, and has been for nearly ever since the marriage of the said Rebecca with him. That he is careless and improvident and unfit to be intrusted with money or property, and that your Oratrix distinctly charges the fact of his insolvency as he will be able to show upon the fund hearing of this cause which sum, if paid into the hands of said Manly Keeble will be so used and applied as to totally deprive the said Rebecca and her children for the use thereof, unless prevented by a Decree . . ." (Imagine what this statement would do for a marriage!)

The above Decree was enacted in 1859. In the ensuing years until the filing of the lawsuit in 1867, the two brothers were attempting to protect their separate interests.

Manly and Rebecca were living on a farm, which had been owned by E. Thomas Dunlap. Mr. Dunlap's heir, James Dunlap, had gone to Texas, and Andrew Peery of Blount County had been appointed Executor of the Estate. The purchase price of the farm was to have been $1,200.00. Rebecca wanted her inheritance to pay a portion of the purchase price. She asked Richard Keeble, her brother-in-law, if he would get her money the next time he was down in Monroe County. He agreed to do so.

Richard makes the trip (no small distance in that day) and buys slaves, as well as other property, from the estate so that he is indebted to the estate some $5,000.00. Executor Griffith, instead of giving Richard money to bring Rebecca, fills out an Order directing Richard to pay $500.00 to Rebecca from what he owes the estate. Richard gives Rebecca the Order, as he did not have $500.00 in hand at this time. Rebecca needs the money for the Dunlap place, having promised Andrew Peery she would pay him from first revenues from the estate. She requests that Richard pay her as soon as possible.

Richard is a man of financial worth. He borrows $500.00 in Confederate money from a Mr. Kennedy, a money lender, in order to satisfy Rebecca. Prior to receiving this species of money, he went to Mr. Peery, knowing the purpose Rebecca wanted it for, and asked Peery if he would accept Confederate money from Rebecca in partial purchase of the Dunlap place. Peery agrees to accept the money. He states that he knows how to get rid of it; he will send it to James Dunlap, the Rebel, who has gone to Texas. Richard borrows the money and delivers it to Manly and his son on December 19, 1862, at the home of Richard's daughter, Margaret Coulter. Manly does not want to accept Confederate currency.

He requests Greenbacks. Richard advises his brother that he has talked to Peery has agreed to accept the southern currency. Manly takes the money with the understanding that if Perry won't accept it, Richard will take it back. They part with that understanding, family members in attendance to hear the promise.

Manly goes straightway through the woods and fields to pay Mr. Peery. In the time since Peery has talked to Richard, he has had a change of mind. He has no way of sending the money to Texas to the heir, and he doesn't want the money on hand should scavengers come through the area and rob him. Peery refuses to accept the money from Manly.

Within the time agreed upon, Manly meets Richard by chance "Just above Perkin's Shop or below the Meeting House" and asks to return the money, which he was carrying on his person. Richard refuses to accept it. He advises Manly to take the money to Maryville and buy salt from the county government. He can then resell the salt for Greenbacks, as Richard himself had done.

Rather than have a quarrel in the family, Manly goes to Maryville where he succeeds in disposing of about $115.00 of the money for salt.

Unfortunately, when he sells the salt, he is given Tennessee State currency, which is just as worthless as the Confederate currency.

The file is full of depositions of family members, all relating what they had seen or heard of the transactions among the brothers and Mr. Peery. It is wartime – what to do with $500.00 in Confederate bills? For a time, Manly and Rebecca each carried half the money in their pockets. When Rebel troops came near, they decided to hide it in a hollow log. The money got wet and damp, and the outer bills had to be replaced to make up the full $500.00. They desire to return the money to Richard. On March 4, 1864, Rebecca dies. Manly becomes Executor of her Estate in Blount County, which completely nullifies the agreement made in 1859 in Monroe County.

Manly still has the money wrapped up and on hand. Now as Executor, he returns to brother Richard and asks him to arbitrate. Richard wants to know what he wants to arbitrate. Marion, son of Richard, was present at this discussion and says in his deposition: "Manly finally ceased talking. Father speaking to Manly says, 'are you through, Manly?' Manly answered 'I am.' Father said, 'what did I ever owe you?' Manly's answer was 'nothing." Father said 'what did you ever know me to owe your wife?' Manly answered 'nothing.' Richard said 'what do you want me to arbitrate?' Manly said, 'this Confederate money you paid to me.' Richard said, 'I have nothing more to do with it.' Richard's next question was 'why did SHE not trade off her Confederate money as I did for salt and turn it into good money?' Manly said "I did buy salt with it to the amount of $115.00 in old State money which is now dead on our hands.' Richard then said, 'I only borrowed the Confederate money from Kennedy as an accommodation to your wife and have had to pay five hundred dollars in Greenbacks in place of it and shall have nothing more to do with it.' Manly then said, 'if we can't arbitrate or settle the matter ourselves, I know who can.'" Now the war is over. Confederate money is completely worthless. Courts have not been held during the war, and litigation has been impossible. As soon as civil government is reestablished, Manly brings suit in Chancery Court in Blount County for redress.

Now a deposition is taken from Richard, and we see another side of the quarrel. "Rebecca Keeble sent me a note by her son Pleas and she said to bring her three hundred dollars from Griffith. I told her if Griffith would sent it, I would bring it. Her son said leave the money at James Colters and she afterwards got the money as she told me. After this I let her have $500.00

at one time, and in a short time I gave her $42.50 which Griffith said was the interest which had been sent by Griffith to her by me. The $42.50 was Confederate Money. The $500.00 was Confederate Money and Bonds. I think it was November 1862. The way I let her have the money was about as follows: I was owing Griffith a large amount of money for slaves purchased from him. Rebecca Keeble had the amount of $500.00 coming to her from her father's estate. Griffith was the Executor of her father's estate and Griffith sent an Order to Rebecca Keeble on me – for $500.00. When Rebecca presented the Order, I did not accept the Order and told her to take it back and the matter stood this way until after I had paid Griffith up all but a very little amount. I went down to settle up with him and while there I asked Griffith if he had paid Rebecca Keeble. He said not and said he would not pay her, that he had given her the Order on me and she had receipted him for it and that was over now. I told him that he not ought to treat her that way, that he ought to pay her and he finally agreed to pay her $500.00 in Confederate Money if she would bring him or send him the Order he had given her and for me to tell her what he would do. When I came home, I told her what Griffith had said. She requested me to assist her in going down after the money. I went down to make a final settlement with Griffith of his matters and mine, but the matter passes on for sometime and we didn't get off to go down to see Griffith to get the money because it being squally times.

I told her, or Manly to tell her, Kennedy had Confederate Money and would loan them money until they could get down and get theirs from Griffith. Manly said Kennedy would not loan them money. I told him I would vouch for her to Kennedy for the amount of the Order. Manly insisted on me to go to Kennedy and get the money for them and hold the order Griffith gave Rebecca until they got their money from Griffith. I at first refused to go to Kennedy for the money for them. The money was Confederate Money and Bonds that I got from Kennedy and I left it at Margaret Colters for Rebecca Keeble as Manly had ordered. I told Margaret to tell Rebecca Keeble if she didn't like the Confederate BONDS to bring them to town the next day and Kennedy would give her Confederate Money for them. The $42.50 I gave her myself was the interest on the $500.00 as Griffith told me. When I gave it to her she thanked me and said she owed me a hundred favors if she never got them paid, 'for you are all the friend I have got on earth' and I never saw or heard anything more about the Order or money until after Rebecca's death. I never owed her anything in my life, nor Manly. What I done was just for an accommodation for the woman as she was my sister-in-law."

In cross examination, Richard states that he is no scholar and can't read himself, and he supposed the document he was given by Sam Keeble (Rebecca's son) was the Order. He knew it was the Order when he returned it to Griffith and was told that it was the proper document.

The final Decree on the suit was rendered on June 11, 1874. The honorable M. L. Hall, Chancellor, was pleased to Order, Adjudge, and Decree that Manly Keeble, Administrator Of the Estate of Rebecca Keeble, deceased, have and recover of Richard Keeble the sum of $649.00 and all the cost of this cause, including interest.

Defendant Richard Keeble prays an appeal from said Decree to the next term of the Supreme Court of Tennessee at Knoxville, Tennessee, to be "holden" on the second Monday of September, next, which appeal is granted the Defendant having executed an appeal bond.

Supreme Court of Tennessee
Knoxville, Tennessee

Volume 1874 – 1875 – 1876, Page 158   October 17, 1874
It appearing to the Court that there is no error in the Decree of the Chancellor, the same is in all things affirmed. The Court is therefore pleased to Order, Adjudge, and Decree that the Complainant Manly Keeble Admr., of Rebecca Keeble, deceased, have and recover of the Defendant Richard Keeble and his Sureties the sum of $663.51 and all the costs of the cause in the Court below and in this Court for which execution is awarded.

Page 275
Manley Keeble vs. Richard Keeble – The Defendant by his Solicitors, enters a motion for a re-hearing which is ordered to be entered and the petition is filed.

Page 296
Manley Keeble vs. Richard Keeble – The motion for a re-hearing in his case is upon due consideration by the Court dis-allowed and the petition dismissed.

Page 309
Manley Keeble vs. Richard Keeble – On motion it is Ordered that the Decree here-to-fore entered during the present term as the final Decree in this case is modified as to make the Solicitors and Richard Keeble jointly obligated for the Court Costs of $250.00 plus interest from the date of the Decree, that being the amount of the appeal Bond executed by the Solicitors, as sureties for said Defendant . . .

A personal note:
An element of Pathos runs undercurrent throughout this suit. As I alluded to on page 216, the necessity of Rebecca withholding her inheritance from her husband caused friction within the family.

The statement of Rebecca, as quoted by Richard, "she thanked me and said she owed me a hundred favors if she never got them paid, for you are all the friend I have got on the earth" certainly expresses her lament of her circumstances.

Manly's comment, when asked by his attorney about the money, "was it of any benefit to you or your wife Rebecca Keeble?" "I never put my hand on a dollar of the money. What I got from Dick for the purpose of using it, nor did it ever do me or my wife Rebecca any good, but a great deal of harm."

Certainly, a bitterness remained between the two brothers, Richard and Manly. Richard's attempt to reverse the judgment, even after appeal to the Supreme Court had been denied, reflects a severe rift in their relationship. The judgment still had not been paid to Manly.

Mr. Edgar "Si" Keeble, grandson of Manly, stated to me that he never knew his grandfather to own any property. When I advised him that Manly had sold property, he wanted to see the Deed. "Si" said that it was common knowledge throughout the family that Manly was not a financial wizard. The land he sold was what he inherited from his father's estate and was sold in 1858.

PLEASANT MARION KEEBLE

Mr. Edgar "Si" Keeble, last surviving son of Pleasant Marion Keeble, was very proud of his father's accomplishments. Indeed, we are all benefited by "Pleas's" labor in placing tombstones on the graves of so many of his and our ancestors.

Mr. Pleas was the last surviving veteran of the ill-fated Sultana disaster and was the central figure in the 65th anniversary of the tragedy.

In a Knoxville newspaper describing Mr. Keeble as a "brisk little man with a big gray mustache," he was then 84 years old, but the paper states "to see him you'd probably, off-hand, call that a lie by 20 years. Studying his firm face and steady eye, you wouldn't allow him a day over 65."

In the memorial services each year for those lost on the Sultana and the survivors, flowers were brought to the Gay Street Bridge in Knoxville, and the flowers were tossed to the waters below. Mr. Si Keeble provided us with a picture from the paper of his father with a wreath in his hand preparing to toss it from the bridge.

Si Keeble wanted something of his father's accomplishments to be retained, and he gave me some of his own thoughts on his beloved father. I shall quote a part of what he wrote.

"After my father was discharged from military service, he hired to my uncle Sam Kountz as a helper in his tanyard. I don't know how long he stayed there, but he must have stayed some years. He learned quite a lot about making leather and how to convert it to useful purposes. Apparently he must have made most of the shoes for the older ones of the family. I have worn a number of pairs which he made for me from childhood to young manhood.

About 1869, the KKK was creating a problem, and the state asked for volunteers for a militia to bring them under control. Dad enlisted and was in that service about six months. At this point, I would like to mention something of great interest to me. Sometime before he enlisted for Civil War duty, he went with his father to a neighbor (not very close). When they arrived, there were some children present, among which there was a little girl some 9 or 10 years old. After they left the scene, he told his father that was a girl he intended to marry. September 22, 1870, he married her. She was our mother.

Sometime before marriage, he bought some acreage (I never knew how much) and built a log house. I think it was only one room. Later a lean-to was added but I think by someone else. After five children (Nallie, Will, Jim, John, and Sam) were born and the farm was at least half paid for, due to a faulty deed he lost the farm and all he had paid. I understand a minor heir had not been properly recompensed and either the court or the party from whom the land was purchased would not allow for an adjustment, so he lost everything. My brother Sam was killed by falling from a horse when only four years old.

Many years later, a cousin, Sam Keeble, bought the farm and a number of his children were born in the old house, which is still standing (if it has not been removed in the last few months. Lloyd Keeble owns it and lives in a newer house nearby.

Somehow Dad managed to grow enough food to feed the family and also worked in a neighborhood blacksmith and wagon building shop, which was owned by Mr. Sam McCullough, a cousin by marriage. Their wives were cousins, both McTeers.

I was 30 years old when I left the farm, and the only wagon we had he built before I can remember, and it was still in good condition.

He was one of the best brick and stone masons I ever saw. A stone chimney which he built, probably 100 or more years ago, is still standing some 300 yards south of Prospect Baptist Church in Blount County. He laid many foundations for church and school buildings and built numerous chimneys over a wide area in Blount County, south Knox County, and lower Sevier County.

He was a good carpenter, being able to calculate his angles, lengths, etc., and cut his framing on the ground and it would fit. He rebuilt and enlarged the old house in which I was born. He also built completely the only barn we ever had while I was on the farm. The heavy framing, sills, plates, and connectors were hewn with a broad axe, and they were straight, square, and very smooth. He made most of the smaller implements and tools used on the farm.

To the best of my knowledge, he made all the tables we had, and he also made one of the old time three-corner cupboards, which Will Keeble had when he died. So far, as well as I know, Nell (who is 99 years old) still has it. I would think it would be somewhat valuable now as an antique.

Also, he was somewhat musical. While not during my lifetime, and I do not recall hearing him mention it. I am told that he taught some singing schools.

I will close by saying that if my statements are in error as to actual facts, I assure you it is due to a faulty memory, and there was no intent of misleading anyone."

This was written by Edgar R. (Si) Keeble in April 1975.

Mr. Si Keeble was a humble and unpretentious man, and we appreciated his friendship and warm hospitality. He would be pleased that we featured his father in this way.

JENNIE MAE KEEBLE GREDIG

Her life story, as dictated to Albert W. Dockter, Jr., on occasion of her 90th birthday May 5, 1990.

As I know very little about my early days on this earth, I will have to rely to a great extent on legal documents about those years. My grandfather, William McCutcheon Keeble, and my grandmother, Nancy Jenkins Keeble, were married in Sevier County, Tennessee, on August 14, 1862, by William M. Burnett, a Minister of Gospel.

I know nothing of my other set of grandparents other than to know that they were George Graham and Eliza Dixon Graham. I never remember having seen this couple. I did not know my mother's birth year, but I had heard that my mother had a twin brother who was named Will Graham; sometimes the name is pronounced Grimes. My son-in-law, Al Dockter, contacted my Uncle Will and secured his birth date and thus I knew my mother's natal day. I have heard that these grandparents lived in the Ellejoy Community, but I did not know that for a fact. My father and his brother-in-law to be, W. J. Jenkins, signed a bond for $1250.00 for the purpose of my father's marriage to my mother, as was common at that time.

State of Tennessee
Sevier County

Know all men by these presents that we, Laban Keeble and W. J. Jenkins are held firmly bound into the State of Tennessee in the sum of $1250.00 to be voided on condition that there be no lawful cause to prevent a marriage from being solemnized in the County of Sevier between Laban Keeble and Alice Graham.

Witness our hands and seal this 13th day of January, 1899
Laban Keeble
W. J. Jenkins

I, John Chandler, Clerk of the County Court, County of Sevier, aforesaid by the power in me vested by law do license you and either of you to celebrate the rites of Matrimony between Laban Keeble and Alice Graham.

Given at office in Sevierville the 13th of January, 1899, and of American Independence, one hundred and twenty three years.

John Chandler, Clerk

I Solemnized the Rites of Matrimony between the above named parties on the 15th of January, 1899.

J. B. Walker, Minister of the Gospel

Apparently my Mother and Dad moved into the home place of my grandmother, Nancy Jenkins Keeble, for when the United States Census was taken in 1900 in November, I was six months old. My father, according to their record, was born in September 1873, but that is incorrect. My father was born on October 12, 1879, and was 21 years of age when he married my mother. The Census states that both of his parents were born in Tennessee, as was he. My mother was listed as Martha A. Keeble. I never heard her called anything but Alice, which was apparently her middle name. This record states that she was 23 years old, having been born in May of 1877. Uncle Will gave their birth dates as May 27, 1877. My mother stated that she and her parents were all born in Tennessee.

Living in the home with us was my grandmother, Nancy Jenkins Keeble, who by the Census record was born in April of 1848. Family records give her birth year as 1843. Nancy stated that she was born in North Carolina. Her parents' names were Caleb and Jane Gibson Jenkins. She had borne eleven children, eight of whom were living at the time the Census was taken.

Also living in the home, or at least staying there at the time of the Census, were Issac M. Keeble (age 4), born March 1896 and listed as a nephew, and Garmon Cattlett (age 1), born in August of 1898 and also listed as a nephew.

My grandmother was listed as the landowner and my Dad as a renter. My grandfather, William McCutcheon Keeble, had died May 9, 1895, just five years before this time. The land we were living on had been a part of the Caleb Jenkins estate, and a portion of the estate was left to my grandmother, his daughter, in his Will dated September 16, 1892.

196

Aunt Polly Keeble Helton, my father's sister, stated that her father and mother's land consisted of some thirty acres in size and was located in the 10th District of Sevier County, approximately five miles from Sevierville. Aunt Polly said that there were some "hard feelings" over the Will, as her father, William McCutcheon, had worked and paid his father-in-law for the land that Nancy was to inherit. A Deed was never given for his payment, but in the Will, it appeared that it was Nancy and Caleb's gift from her father. Other members of the family inherited their part without any effort on their part, while Nancy received what had been paid for and nothing more. Polly said, "My father's last payment on the land was a yoke of oxen, which I remember him paying and the great satisfaction he felt upon being out of debt. Grandpa kept putting off making a Deed to my Dad. Fortunately, the Will was made so that Mother received the land at all, but the land had been paid for."

Grandmother sold the land to her youngest brother, William J. (Jepp) Jenkins, in March of 1902 or 1903 and moved to Kansas.

I was born some sixteen months after my parents married; and sometime during that time, my mother contracted tuberculosis. Mother died on February 23, 1901, when I was but nine months old. She was buried at Pleasant Hill Methodist Church Cemetery in Sevier County, Tennessee. One of the few things I remember my father saying about my mother was that he had never heard her make an unkind remark about anyone.

Dad must have been lonely; and after seeing my mother gradually fade away and with a child to care for and support, he found a helpmate. On September 21, 1901, just seven months after my mother's death, he married Catherine Garner, daughter of Francis Garner and Sarah C. Davis Garner in Blount County, Tennessee.

Aunt Polly said grandmother sold her farm to Jepp Jenkins in March of 1902 or 1903, so I would assume that was when we moved to Kansas. The year was probably 1903, for Alice (my sister) was born in October of 1902, and I know that she went to Kansas with us. I, of course, was too young to remember living in Tennessee, and my first recollections are of living in Anthony, Kansas. Nancy Keeble was living with us.

197

Dad had a job with the railroad. I have no idea what railroad line or what his task was. Later he was employed in a salt plant. I know nothing of that work either.

Three of my father's sisters and his brother and their families also moved to Kansas. Susan Headrick, Rindy Clinton, Prudy Floyd, and Caleb Keeble all went from Tennessee, and so most of the family was together at that time. The families all moved to Kansas by train.

I had never known my birth mother, and so it was natural for me to love and cherish Mom as my own, along with the other children n the family.

In the fall of 1905, my grandmother and I boarded the train for Tennessee to visit our relatives. I remember the trip vividly. We stayed with Aunt Adeline and Uncle "Rich" Floyd in Sevier County. My brother Kenneth was born in Kansas in August 1905 while my grandmother and I were in Tennessee. After a good visit, we boarded the train again for Kansas.

While grandmother lived with us in Kansas, she wouldn't let my parents cut my hair. It was red, the color of her own hair. My hair was thick, and I had two braids in the front, and they joined the other braids in the back. Grandma brushed my hair every day. It was down to my waist or longer.

I went to the first and second grades in Anthony and hadn't finished second grade when we returned to Tennessee to live. My first grade teacher was Miss Davies. My second grade teacher was Anna Davies. I contracted scarlet fever in June 1907 and grandmother cared for me. No one in the family was allowed to come into my room except grandma. They were afraid that Anderson, our new baby, and me might get scarlet fever. I am sure I contracted it at school.

I would judge that it was November or December 1907-08 when we returned to Tennessee. Anderson was born in June 1907, and we came home after his birth. My father said that he thought Tennessee would be a better place to raise his family than in the city of Anthony, but I liked the school there. I have a picture of my classmates at the Anthony School where I attended. Two of my cousins are in the picture, also Mattie Headrick and Bill Clinton.

Grandmother stayed in Kansas when Dad and Mom brought their family home to Tennessee. She died there in about 1920, the year Bill and I married. When visiting Aunt Rindy Clinton in California in 1932, she said "Mae, you'll never know how much your grandmother loved you." Apparently my return east with the family grieved her deeply.

I want to say here and now before I go on with my story that mother never treated me any differently than any of the other children. When she made a dress for Alice, she made a dress for me. There was never a time that I remember of feeling unloved or discriminated against in any way. Mom had enough love for us all, and I felt as if I were her child, as I had no other mother.

I remember thinking when we got back to Tennessee that this was the most God forsaken place I had ever seen. I had liked the city life of Anthony. The train brought us (Alice, Kenneth, Anderson, Mom, Dad, and I) to Melrose Station up near Walland, Blount County, Tennessee. Grandpa Garner was there to meet us with a large team of horses and a large wagon. We put all our belongings into the wagon, which included a sewing machine that Dad had bought for Mom in Kansas. I don't remember whether we brought much furniture or not. We then all climbed into the wagon.

It was necessary to cross Little River to get to Grandpa Garner's home, and so he drove the team down below the dam at Peerys' Mill to a place where the riverbanks were sloped enough for a team and wagon to enter the water, cross the river, and ascend the bank on the other side. The water was shallow at this site, at least shallow enough to keep the contents of the wagon dry.

I remember, as we cross the river and saw the wagon wheels raise up over those big smooth round rocks and then drop back down into the water, asking my father if the water made those big round rocks. I had not seen a river before that looked like this one. We went home with grandpa and Grandma Garner, while Dad looked for a place to buy to take his family. Dad was able to find a small place, which he bought from Steve Graves. The price was $400.00, and Dad paid for it in cash.

A funny thing happened while we were staying with Grandpa Garner; it seems funny to me now anyway. Grandma Garner had false teeth. I ran to

Dad and told him that Grandma Garner had taken her teeth out and washed them and that I was going to do the same with mine! I am sure Dad chuckled at that one!

Our new home was up near Old Chilhowee Church in Blount County. It was rather isolated but was a big log house with a fireplace as large as my present breakfast nook. The fireplace was of mountain rock. The kitchen was off to one side of the house, and a big bedroom was off the other side of the house. The bedroom had been added to the house before we owned it. You had to step down one step from the floor level and through a door into the bedroom. Our beds were lined up along the back wall and each of us knew where our bed was.

There was a spring near the house from which we got our water supply. The house was on a rocky road with streams to ford. Buggies and horses could get to the old place, but it would have been impossible to get a car in there, had we owned one.

When we first arrived at our new home, I marveled at the beauty of the trees all around our home. The fire flies were so thick! I had never seen them before and it being the fall of the year, I was afraid they would set the dry leaves on fire and we and our new home would be consumed by the flames.

Dad took care of the fireplace. There was a regular ritual about its care, especially at night. First of all, he would put what we called a "back stick" at the rear of the fireplace. This "stick," as we called it, was in reality a large half section of a beech or oak log. These two woods, because of their density of grain, burned slowly and by being at the rear of the fireplace, they thrust the heat from the fire burning in front out into the room and made the fireplace much more energy efficient. Just one large back stick was used at a time, but having the back sticks available for use required much sawing and splitting of these hard woods.

At night Dad would cover up the smaller burning logs in front of the back stick with ashes. He wanted the fire to smolder through the night. Putting ashes on the fire took oxygen away and made the fire burn more slowly

First thing in the morning he would stir up the logs, move the ashes off the logs, add some heart of pine chips, which contained a lot of rosin and thus burned quickly into a flame, and reestablished the fire for another day.

There was a fine orchard near the house. We had early red June apples, horse apples that were yellow and almost grapefruit sized and Cheese apples that were a dark yellow color like cheese were a medium-sized apple. We canned everything, made jellies, jams, and preserves. We canned peas, beans, corn and most of the garden vegetables. We were never hungry. We had milk cows so we had cream and butter; we had hogs so we had hams, lard, sausage, and bacon; and through it all (gardening, harvesting, and all), I never heard Mama complain about anything.

We lived within a mile of the Old Chilhowee Baptist Church, and we attended there. The minister tried to get Dad to join the church, but he wouldn't because they had "closed Communion." My father told the minister that if he joined and his mother came with him to church on that Sunday, Communion Sunday, she would not be allowed to take Communion with him and that he would not join for that reason. The minister agreed that would be the situation.

Grandmother did visit us while we lived at Old Chilhowee when she made yet another trip east to visit her loved ones here.

Dad told us that the children of the community were making fun of our Kansas accent. The local children sounded funny to me.

I was never in my life called a step child, and I recall only one time that my father took me aside when I was seven or eight years old and said, "I want you to be a good girl and be kind to Mom. She loves you like the other children." That was the only remark ever made to me by him regarding my status in the family.

Leonard and Clyde were born while we lived at old Chilhowee. We went to school for four years while living there. The school was near the church. It was the end of the school year when we were living with Grandpa Garner. Mama had a younger sister, Ola, who was in the first grade. Even though I would have been in the second or third grade, I wanted to go to school and class with Ola. It was the end of the school year, so they permitted it; and so just for that few weeks, I felt comfortable in the first grade with Ola. My teacher was Lizzie Davis.

Years later when I attended Rex Davis and Marilyn Keeble's wedding at Eucebia Church, Lizzie and her sisters, Emma and Evelyn Davis, attended. Lizzie said to me "Mae, you were a nice little girl. You always came to school so clean and you always had a clean mind." Emma Davis, Miss Lizzie's sister, was my third grade teacher. Luther Rogers taught the fourth grade, I believe.

The school had a wooden exterior. It had a pot-bellied stove in the center of the room; and when it was really cold, we all hovered around the stove. The windows were all along the outside walls, and so it was cold over there during the winter. There was no running water in the building. There was a well (not a cistern), and we all used the same dipper from a bucket of water on the table at the rear of the classroom. We became concerned about germs and soon brought our own cups for drinking water. There were two outhouses at opposite ends of the playground, one for boys and one for girls.

The minister at the Old Chilhowee Church while we lived there was a Reverend Tittsworth part of the time. George Garner, Sr., was the song leader; and since the church did not have a piano or organ, Mr. Garner used a tuning fork to get a tone for us to start a hymn.

We then moved to Cold Springs Road down below Keeble Chapel. There we had a four-room boxed house. The old road ran near the house, but the present road it built quite a distance up the hill and away from the house. We had a well at this residence but continued to use oil lamps for lighting. Here the remainder of my brothers and sisters were born – Charles, Nita, Joe, Jim, and Ella.

There were two schools available to us at this new home, Rocky Branch School and Cold Springs School. Dad sent us to whichever school he thought had the best teacher. In any case, we walked to school two miles each way. The school year lasted about six months. At that time, there was no high school in Blount County except Porter Academy. At Rocky Branch School, Mr. Marcel ("Cell") Millsaps was the teacher. I do not know what his educational background was.

It was while attending this school that I first met Bill Gredig. He was working for Mr. Sam Ogle, who had a sawmill. Bill would come home to Ogles in the morning and wait for Mr. Ogle to get ready to go to work. I was at the school playgrounds, and we would talk across the fence.

About 1912-1914, I joined the Walkers Chapel Methodist Church. Bill attended there also. Even after moving to Maryville, we drove back up to Walkers Chapel to church on Sundays.

I remember that the church was trying to raise money to purchase a bell for the belfry. Bill and I were dating some, and the church had a pie supper in which the girls made pies and the fellows bid on their girlfriend's pies. I had brought a chocolate pie, and Bill had to bid $7.75 to get that pie. My father said that it must have been a good pie to pay that price for it.

We raised the money for the bell, and it is interesting to note that when Walkers Chapel was torn down and the members went to Walland Methodist Church, the bell was taken up there and installed in their church. The timbers and siding of the Walkers Chapel Church were used to enlarge the Walland Church also.

We attended Walkers Chapel until about 1935, when we joined First Methodist Church in Maryville. All that remains at the site of Walkers Chapel now is the cemetery located on the hillside with its grave markers.

After graduating from Rocky Branch School, Alice and I went to Maryville College Prep. School. Alice, Ola McCampbell, and I roomed together at the college. One of my teachers had been Ella McCampbell, a graduate of Maryville College in 1913. I learned more from her in two years than I had learned from anyone else in all my schooling. It was through her influence that Ola McCampbell, Alice, and I roomed together. Those classes would have been about 1917-1918.

We rode the train from Melrose Station on Monday morning to Maryville, stayed in the dorm all week, and returned home by train on Saturday mornings. It is interesting to remember that in those days riding on the train, we crossed over land that Bill and I have owned for 55 years. The railroad has been gone since the thirties, but the roadbed and grading are mute evidence of the once-busy line.

By this time, Dad had a touring car, and the older boys went to Porter High. Anderson, Kenneth, and Clyde went to Porter for four years. Leonard went three years and then left to get a job.

Nita graduated from Walland High School, then Mom and Dad moved to a farm in the Friendsville area. Jim and Ella graduated from Friendsville High. I can't remember if Joe graduated from Porter or Walland.

I took a teacher's exam at the Blount County Courthouse and passed the exam, giving me the credentials to teach in the grade schools of Blount County. I was assigned to a school "in the Canes," which was located up in the mountains above Walland. My Dad hitched up old "Lue" to a buggy and took me up there. He would come for me once a month on Friday and take me home for a weekend. We would return to the Canes again on Sunday afternoon. It was a terribly lonely existence there.

I roomed with Mae Gourley's parents, John and Esther Buchanan. I paid them $12.00 a month board and room. I earned $37.50 a month salary. I was the teacher in a one-room school with about 20 to 25 students. My pupils were mostly from the Cooper, Sellers, and Buchanan families. Since I was earning money and was able to save it living there, I was able to pay for a second year at Maryville College Prep. School.

In 1919 I was appointed to Cold Springs School to teach. It was a two-room school, and I had the first three grades to teach. Hubert Tipton had the other three grades. His father was John Newton Tipton. There I made $40.00 a month. Here I was able to live at home and walk the two miles to school in the mornings. It was so much more satisfactory being with my family again after being isolated in the Canes. Here the students were all ages; three of them were my age. I had about 35 pupils in the three grades. At this school there was a spring nearby for our water. We each had our own cups for drinking. The school had the two outhouses at opposite ends of the playground.

Bill had been gone to World War I for two years, 1916-1918. I was teaching up in the "Canes" when I learned that he had been wounded. A nurse caring for him at Walter Reed Hospital in Washington, DC, wrote me a letter and told me that Bill was in serious condition. I didn't think that I would ever see him again. I later learned that the same shell that killed

Captain Lonas had been responsible for Bill losing his leg and for the shrapnel that was embedded over his body.

Bill was confined to Walter Reed Hospital for about a year. When he was able to come home for a furlough, he came by our house and got old "Lue" and rode him to his home. His brother, Frank, brought the horse back home.

In November 1919 Bill was discharged, and Clyde (a 9-year old) drove the horse and wagon down to Melrose Station to get Bill and took him to his home. We were married in July of 1920 by Stanley "Skeeter" Shields' father, who was a Justice of the Peace (Jim Shields).

My father had misgivings about our marriage, feeling that Bill would never be able to make a living in his crippled condition and that I would be forced to be the bread winner. Several times in later life, he admitted how wrong he had been and told me what a fine husband I had and what a fine son-in-law he had.

We started housekeeping in a two-room house up near Perrys Mill. Dad was working in the Mill for the Perrys, and they hired Bill. We stayed there about a year. There was a lot of climbing to do up and down stairs to see about the milling of the grains. The steps were very narrow because of their steep ascent; and with a cumbersome wooden leg, it was dangerous. The dust and the climbing brought on a weakening of Bill's condition and so we moved to Maryville.

Here we lived for about five months in a little house on the corner of Sevierville Road and Washington Avenue, then we built a 4-room house on McAdams Street, of which we were very proud.

At this time, Bill was in Vocational Training with the government and was paid $135.00 for pension and training. He learned the cobbler's trade. Bill concluded the training and bought a shop already in existence on Washington Avenue on a site where Laws Furniture Store is now located. One of my brothers was very young, and he told everyone that Bill was a Shoe Gobbler.

After about a year in the Shoe Shop, Bill's cough reappeared, and he had to get away from the dust and the hum of the machinery that wore on his nerves. We lived at the McAdams Street site for three years and then moved to the house on Sevierville Road where Onnie Keeble now resides.

I must backtrack at this point to include something I have left out. Bill and I just walked off from home and got married on July 8, 1920. A day or two later, Alice did the same thing. She walked off from home and married Jake Whitehead, son of Samuel Whitehead and Nancy (Donaldson) Whitehead.

We were living on McAdams Street, and Alice and Jake were living on a little street behind the Lamar Chapel just off Sevierville Road when Dorothy, daughter of Alice and Jake, came to stay with us permanently. Alice and Jake had Elsie and then Dorothy was born. From the time that she first reacted to those around her, Dorothy "took" to her Uncle Bill. We kept her from time to time and enjoyed her company. There was no thought in the beginning that she would come to live with us and be our own. Gradually she stayed with us more and more and finally was with us all the time.

We had bought the house Onnie lives in from John Blevins, and it needed repairs; we lived in Otha Gibson's rental house for two months. It was while we were staying in the rental house that one morning Dorothy called from the living room, "Mommy." From that moment on, I was Mommy and Bill was Daddy in her vocabulary. Dorothy had been born May 15, 1923, and we were in the rental house sometime in the year 1925. She went by the Whitehead name until about the third grade. The children kept quizzing her about why she was a Whitehead and lived with the Gredigs, so she took our name and from then on insisted she was a Gredig.

Bill and I always had ambition for Dotty to have a college education. We had been unable to have the kind of education we wanted and realized the necessity of an education for a more full life, as well as a means of a livelihood. Dotty said, upon graduation from high school, that she knew she had to go to college, as it had been expected of her all her life.

We were extremely proud of her, as she graduated from Everett High School in 1940 as Valedictorian of the Senior Class. She had done well with her piano lessons and played the Processional and Recessional marches for the graduates at Commencement. She played two piano solos and also had a speaking part in the program. Her piano lessons had been started when she started to school, and she played for services at Walkers Chapel before we ever left there for First Church Maryville.

All through high school, she had taken an active part in the Youth Fellowship at First Methodist Church and one year went to Sullins College in Bristol to Summer Conference for Methodist Young People. As you can see, Dorothy was the "apple of our eye;" and as we worked on the farm, she became our expression of hope for the younger generation.

While living at the house where Onnie now lives, we were able to raise chickens. We had a pig, a cow, and a horse. The latter we used to make a garden. We lived there for nine years in what we called Rigsbytown, jokingly called because a Mr. Rigsby had built some of the houses that sat in a row at the site.

The big old farmhouse and farm that had been owned by Andy Dunn was nearby and was for sale by Maryville College. Bill thought that he had been successful in managing the place where we were and wanted to buy the farm. Working with the animals, breathing fresh air, and tilling the soil appealed to him; thus, in 1934 we bought the farm.

Again I must backtrack a little. In 1932 during the depression, Alice and Jake Whitehead and family moved to California. Jake had been employed at Alcoa and was forced to take a cut in pay. Like so many others, Jake took his family to California expecting to find work there, but alas the depression had arrived there also. We were all concerned about their welfare and so Dad, Bill, Dotty, and I drove to California in our four-door 1930 Model "A" Ford to visit them. Bill withdrew a part of our savings from the bank to make the trip.

When we returned home, the banks had closed their doors permanently, and we were always grateful we had made the trip and had used some of the funds we would have lost in the bank failure.

The Dunn house and grounds were in a very poor state of repair when we purchased the property. There was an old barn between the house and what is now called Genesis Street. To the west of the barn was a hog lot. That barn was in sadder condition than our present barn. Where our breakfast nook is was part of the back porch. There was a long hall from the front door to the back porch and doors off the hall to each side.

207

In the field to the east of the house, large gullies had eroded the topsoil away, and we actually had cows from our herd fall down into them and appeared lost. Bill would have to go down and assist them in getting out of the deep recesses.

We started in with determination to make the place a home to be proud of. New hardwood floors were laid throughout the downstairs. A new roof was put on protecting all those gables from the weather. We closed off that long hall through the house and opened archways into the living room and from the dining room to the sun room. The breakfast nook was taken from the back porch and the kitchen modernized with a wall of cabinets, countertops, and new sink. A new furnace was installed and the house rewired.

The old barn near the house was dismantled and became the site of our garden. A new cistern was dug to save rainwater in addition to the one already under the back porch, since at that time the city waterline had not come out of town that far.

Sevierville Road was a piked road, gravel until sometime in the 1940s. We would sit out front under a big elm tree and watch the cars go by. In those days, you knew the folks in about every car that passed. Life was much simpler as far as society went, but the manual labor that we accomplished to restore and keep the property up was tremendous.

We knew all our neighbors well and were pleased with their achievements and were saddened with their sorrows. When they had need, food or help in the fields, we assisted them.

Bill was very proud when he bought a herd of Ayshire cattle from Wisconsin. They were fine milk cows, and he constructed a milking barn with automatic milkers, maintained a cooler, and had the dairy association come for and grade the milk that he sold to them.

We had a large grape vineyard behind the house. Every year we made grape jellies and grape juice for our pleasure. Gradually we added land adjoining our original 20 acres until we had approximately 40 acres. We then owned the land on each side of the railroad so that when the railroad closed in the late 1930s, we became the owners of the railroad bed that ran through our property. We owned only on one side; we received one-half of the roadbed.

When we bought that property, there was a cistern down in the field to the east of the house. Every year jonquils came up near the cistern so that we knew that at sometime there had been a home or cabin there. Also down below the present barn near the creek that runs through the property, there was a well. Bill filled it in to keep someone or cattle from falling into it.

Bill and I were able to celebrate our 50th wedding anniversary at our home in 1970. Family, neighbors, and friends shared the happy occasion with us. We bought a new 4-door Oldsmobile for our present to each other. Bill's health began to deteriorate, and much of the farm work had to be curtailed.

Ever since our trip to California, Bill had enjoyed being a homebody. He had been to Europe during World War I, which was a demoralizing trip, and he had seen America across the land to California in the depression. To him there was no place on earth that could compare with sitting under a tree in his backyard and enjoying the breeze and the company of friends and loved ones. It was there that he spent his declining days, frustrated that he couldn't work but accepting the fact with courage and grace. Bill passed away on Sunday, June 30, 1974. He was buried in Grandview Cemetery, where we had purchased lots years before.

It is now July 1990, and I lived on in the home that over the years came to mean so much to us.

Mrs. Gredig passed away on January 30, 1997.

DR. WILLIAM HOUSTON KEEBLE
(1873 - 1963)

Dr. Keeble, who I mentioned numerous times in this book, was a distinguished Professor of Physics at Randolph-Macon College from 1919 until his retirement in 1952. He was a native of Blount County, Tennessee. He studied at Maryville College and at the University of Tennessee, where he received a Bachelor of Science degree in 1903. He did graduate work at Columbia University and the University of Chicago, where he worked with 1923 Nobel Laureate Dr. Robert A. Millikan.

He was awarded an honorary Doctor of Science degree by Maryville College in 1945. Before going to Randolph-Macon College, he was Professor of Physics at the College of William and Mary from 1907 to 1919.

Dr. Keeble was a member of Phi Beta Kappa, the American Physical Society, the American Association of Physics Teachers, the American Astronomical Society, and was a Fellow of the American Association for the Advancement of Science.

Construction of the Keeble Observatory building was initiated to house a 12-inch Newtonian Telescope built and donated in 1960 by Foy N. Hibbard, a former director of the United States Weather Bureau in Richmond, Virginia. The dome was completed, and the Hibbard was first used in 1963. The present Cassegrain telescope was purchased from Tinsley Foundation in 1966. In 1988, the telescope drive was completely replaced during renovations, which also included raising the telescope's pier and rebuilding the observation platform.

The Keeble Observatory is a teaching laboratory of the Physics Department of Randolph-Macon College in Ashland, Virginia. Its facilities are used by students in the college's astronomy courses and by advanced physics students with an interest in astronomy. The Observatory is a cornerstone instrument in the college's minor program in astrophysics. The Observatory is located on the college campus, which is approximately 15 miles north of Richmond, Virginia.

The above information was derived from Keeble Observatory literature available to visitors at Randolph-Macon College campus, Ashland, Virginia.

WILLIAM KEEBLE WILL
1727 – Somerset County, Maryland

In the name of God, Amen: I, William Kibble of Somerset County, being very sick and weak of body, but of perfect mind and memory thanks be to God therefore yet calling to mind the mortality of the body and knowing that it is appointment for all men once to die and after death to Judgment do make this my last Will and Testament in form following First and principally I give and bequeath my Soul unto the hands of Almighty God that first gave it to me and my body I commit to the earth from whence it came to be decently buried at the discretion of my Executrix hereafter named trusting that at the general resurrection of the dead, I shall receive the same through the merits of my blessed Lord and Savior Jesus Christ and as touching such worldly goods as it hath pleased God to bless me with I leave as follows: viz.

1st. I give and bequeath to my eldest son John Kibble eighty acres of land being where he did live, that is to say, beginning at the Riverside and running parallel with the upper line of my tract of land alienated to me by Richard Stevens and John Stevens till it intersects the back line that comes from Wicomico Creek being part of said Tract to him and the heirs of his body lawfully begotten forever but in case my said son John Kibble die without such heir then the said eighty acres of land to him so bequeathed to the proper right of my son Richard Kibble and his heirs and assigns forever.

2nd. I give and bequeath unto my son William Kibble the remaining part of my said Tract of Land Alienated to me by Richard and John Stevens to him and his heirs and assigns forever, but not to hinder or debar his mother, my beloved wife of any priviledge of the same during her Widowhood on any pretense whatever.

3rd. I give the third part of my estate after debts and funeral charges are paid to my beloved wife Usly Kibble and to her disposal.

4th. I give the rest of my estate to be equally divided amongst my Seven Children Viz: John Kibble, Abigail Kibble, William Kibble, Ann Kibble, Mary Kibble, Sarah Kibble, and Richard Kibble.

And lastly, I appoint my well beloved wife Usly Kibble to be whole and Sole Executrix Of this my last will and testament revoking all other and former Wills by me made ratifying and allowing what shall be done by my Executrix in Testimony hereof I have set my hand and fixt my seal this 24th day of April Anno Dom 1727.

Signed, sealed, and published and pronounced in presence of us

John Stevens   Robert Mallone   George Dashiell

(At the foot of the foregoing Will was the following Probate's Note)

April the 2nd came George Dashiell and Robert Mallone two of the three subscribers evidence to the above Will and made oath on the Holy Evangels of Almighty God that they saw the Testator William Kibble sign and seal and heard him publish, pronounce and declare the above instrument of writing to be his last Will and Testament and at the time of his doing so to the best of their understanding of sound and disposing mind, memory and understanding and that they, the aforesaid George Dashiell and Robert Mallone subscribed this Will and further saith that they saw the other evidence of John Stevens sign at the same time, all in the presence and at the request of the Testator William Kibble, Sworn before me Nehemiah King Depty Com.ey of Somerset County.

WILLIAM KEBLE, SR., WILL – June 28, 1770

In the name of God Amen. I William Keble, Sen. Of Somerset County in the Province of Maryland, Planter, knowing that it is appointed for all men to die and being weak of body but of sound mind and memory do expose of the worldly estate where with it hath pleased Almighty God to bless me in the following manner to wit:

1st. I order and will that all my just debts be paid off and satisfied.

2nd. Whereas I gave a Bond sometime past to my son George Keble for the Conveyance of the Land where I now live and some lands on the head of said Tract that I took up to prevent any disputes that may arise touching the Validity of said Bond, I do leave the lands, Houses, Orchard, with all other Appurtenances where I now live with the Lands taken up at the back of Joseph Morris's and Thomas Collin's to my said son George Keble and his heirs forever and in case my said son George die without issue than the above lands go to my youngest son John Keble and his heirs forever.

3rd. I leave the lands I had by my wife with the remainder of my lands not already devised to my son William Keble and his heirs forever.

4th. I will and desire that my personal estate where with it hath pleased God to bless me, be appraised by my friends Messr's Thomas and George Dashiell and be equally divided between my sons William Keble, George Keble, John Keble, and my daughters Ann Malow and Sara Keble with the reservation of the payment of my debts as above and the reservation of one nett third part thereof with the third part of all my lands which I leave to my Beloved wife Hannah Keble.

Lastly, I will and appoint my well beloved son George Keble whole and sole Executor to this my Last Will and Testament and so devise that after the Appraisment as above ordered of the Division be made as above to my Wife and Children. I desire that my son George may take that part of my estate which will be the right of my son John and give his Bond to the said Appraisers for the re-payment of it when my said son John becomes of Age and further I desire that my son George will take care of my said son til he be fitt to bind out to Business at which time its my request and I hereby empower my said son George to bind the said John out to such Business that he with the advice of my friends Thomas Dashiell, George Dashiell and

Henry Lowes may think best for him, and I do hereby revoke and utterly dis annual all and every other Will and Wills here-to-fore made by me hereby declaring and pronouncing this to be my last Will and Testament.

In Witness where of I have hereto sett my hand and seal this 28th Day of June A.D. 1770.

William (X) Keble

Signed Sealed and Declared and pronounced in presence of

Henry Lowes   Ann Steuart   Mary Riglands

On the back of the foregoing Will was thus written Viz: On the 4th Day of May 1771 came Henry Lowes and made oath on the Holy Evangelist of Almighty God the within Instrument of writing is the true and only Will and Testament of William Keble, Late of Somerset County deceased that hath come to his hands of possession and that he did not know or ever heard of any other.

Sworn before Thos. Holbrook, Depty. Com.ry.

GEORGE KIBBLE WILL – September 8, 1775

In the name of God Amen and as touching such worldly Estate where with God has been pleased to bless me in this life. I give devise and dispose of the same in the following manner and form.

1st. I give and bequeath to Mary, my Beloved Wife the whole of my Estate to bring up my son as long as she remaineth my Widow, and if she marry then to have only her third, and likewise to pay my Beloved Brother John Kibble, his part out of the Estate when he comes to the age of twenty-one years and to James Bounds fifty pounds, as well as my just debts and then the Land and Tenaments to defend to my well beloved son George Kibble, likewise. In constitute make and ordain Mary, My Wife to be sole Executrix of this my Last Will and Testament all and Singular Truly to possess and enjoy as no other to be my Last Will and Testament.

In Witness thereof I have here unto set my hand and Seal the 8th of September in the year of our Lord One Thousand Seven Hundred and Seventy Five.

George Kibble

Signed, Sealed and Published, Pronounced and Declared in the presence of us:

Robert Mallone   John Wallston   Thomas Nelson

(On the back of the foregoing Will was written) Viz:

October 19, 1775, then came Mary Kibble and made oath that the within instrument of writing is the true and whole Will and Testament of George Kibble, late of Somerset County, deceased that hath come to her hands or possession and that she hath not known of any other

Certified Thos. Holbrook Dy Comm. Of Somerset County

Somerset County October 19, 1775, then came Robert Mallone two of the subscribing witnesses to the within last Will and Testament of George Kibble late of Somerset County, Dec'd. and favorable made oath on the Holy Evangels of Almighty God, that they did see the Testator therein named sign and seal this Will and that they heard him publish, pronounce and declare the same to be his Last Will and Testament, at the time of his doing so he was to the best of their apprehensions of a sound and disposing mind memory and understanding and they respectively subscribed their names as witnesses to this Will in the presence of the testator and in the presence of each other and they also made oath that they did not see Thomas Nelson the other subscribing witness subscribed his name as witness to the said Will in the presence of said deceased.

Certified by Thomas Holbrook Deputy Comm. For Somerset County

INDEX

225

Name	Page
Stone, Martha Ellen	104
Stones, J.	67
Stuart, Jeb	178-179,180, 182
Summey, Jim	83
Sutton, William	28-30
Taff, William	33
Tarwater, Nancy Ellen Floyd	17, 175
Taylor, A. L.	67
Taylor, D.	68
Taylor, James	134
Taylor, John	134
Taylor, Zach	27
Tedford, Robert A.	59, 61, 63-65
Tedford, R. E.	76-77, 155
Templin, David H.	3
Thompson, Matilda	124
Thompson, Samuel	79
Thornton, John	27
Thornton, Reuben	27
Tipton, Captain	70
Tipton, C. P.	106
Tipton, Hubert	204
Tipton, John Newton	204
Tittsworth, Rev.	202
Toliver, Col.	18, 42
Toole, J. E. (Col.)	130
Toole, J. N. & Co.	67
Toole, John E.	70
Townsend, Mary	80, 173-175
Turk, James	42-44
Utterback, Ben J.	27
Varnell, Wm.	164
Waddle, William	27m 141
Walker, Alvin S.	138, 140
Walker, H. H.	140
Walker, Houston	128
Walker, J. B. (Rev.)	196
Walker, James	86, 128-129, 134
Walker, John	33, 134

www.ingramcontent.com/pod-product-compliance
Lightning Source LLC
Chambersburg PA
CBHW080233270326
41926CB00020B/4224